A Second Book of 101 School Assembly Stories

A Second Book of 101 School Assembly Stories

by Frank Carr

LONDON

W. FOULSHAM & CO. LIMITED

NEW YORK TORONTO CAPE TOWN SYDNEY

W. FOULSHAM & CO. LIMITED
Yeovil Road, Slough, Berks., England

Also published by Foulsham:

101 School Assembly Stories

and

A Third Book of 101 School Assembly Stories

ISBN 0-572-01017-6
© Copyright by S. Carney 1981
Artwork © W. Foulsham & Co. Ltd. 1981

Printed and bound in Great Britain at The Bath Press, Avon

Contents

Thematic Index

Acknowledgements

I am indebted to my colleagues Martin Leech and Philip Jones for telling me some of these tales and suggesting the sources of others.

Despite every effort it has not been possible to trace the source of all these stories. If an author's copyright has been infringed sincere regrets are tendered.

The Author and Publishers are grateful for permission to use the following stories in this collection:

The Converted Snake; Chuang Wags his Tail (Routledge & Kegan Paul Ltd):

Timothy Winter; The Camel's Hump; The Heron; The Bells of Heaven; The Swan and the Pike (Macmillan):

The Miser's Bargain (The Miser of Castro – University of Chicago Press):

Father Borrelli (A Street Lamp and the Stars – Peter Davies Ltd).

TRUE STORIES

A Thief Checkmated

If you do not believe the following story you cannot be blamed. It seems most unlikely to be true. Nevertheless it is. Only the names have been changed, for the main characters are still alive.

Some years ago the police of a big city were baffled by a series of expert burglaries. Furs, jewels and other items of great value vanished without trace. The thief left a couple of fingerprints but these did not match any in the police files. It was clear to Inspector Lampitt, who was in charge of the case, that he was dealing with no ordinary crook.

One night he went to his chess club. It was a Tuesday. On that night every week he visited the club to forget his cares over the chess board. He played several games with his friend Lidford, a rich business-man, and afterwards the two men relaxed over a cup of coffee. Lidford chatted for a while about a holiday from which he had just returned and then asked, 'How's the case going?'

'There have been no burglaries for the last few weeks,' replied the detective. Then, laughing, he added: 'It looks as if the thief has been on holiday too.'

Two nights later the robber struck again. This time it was a jeweller's shop and he got away with a splendid haul. Inspector Lampitt was close to despair.

The robbery had been so cleverly done that he wondered if he would ever get his man. He took out his file on the case and read through his papers for the twentieth time. There must, he told himself, be a clue among these papers – something he had overlooked.

An hour later he straightened up, a look of amazement on his face. It's not possible, he thought. He checked his papers again. Yes, not a single burglary had taken place on a night when he was playing chess with Lidford. Tuesday was the only day of the week on which none of the jobs had been pulled. Nor had the thief struck when Lidford was on holiday. He remembered joking about that. But why should someone as well-off as Lidford take to crime? The answer came at once – greed. Some folk are never satisfied with what they've got. But it was all too far-fetched to be true.

During his next visit to the chess club Lampitt drank his customary coffee with Lidford after their game. When they were leaving he secretly slipped his friend's cup into his pocket. Then he drove straight to his office and took the cup to the finger-print expert. After comparing the prints on the cup with those of the thief the expert announced: 'They're the same.'

Some days later Lidford left his house at midnight. A few minutes' walk brought him to the jewellery quarter. He stopped outside a big shop. Carefully he looked up and down the street. There was no one in sight. The only sound he heard was the distant barking of a dog. Within seconds he had let himself in and was kneeling at the safe. Suddenly the light went on and Lampitt stood in the doorway, backed by two uniformed policemen.

Lidford's eyes bulged in astonishment. 'How did you know?'

'The prints on your coffee cup.'

'But, but why didn't you pull me in at the time?'

Lampitt's reply was angry and triumphant. 'Because you made such a fool of me that I just had to catch you in the act.'

Sydney Smith

There are still some folk who think that one cannot be religious and merry. True believers, they will tell you, take their faith so seriously that there is no room for laughter in their lives. Besides, people who joke about *anything* tend to joke about *everything*, even the solemn truths of the great creeds. This notion is dying out nowadays but in Sydney Smith's time it ruled the religious life of the nation.

He was born in Woodford, Essex, in 1771. His quick brain and bubbling good nature helped him survive a wretched schooling at Winchester. After finishing his education at Oxford he became a coun-try curate and carried out his duties diligently, but he longed for the life of the city. When the chance came to go to Edinburgh as a tutor he seized it joyously.

He quickly attracted a circle of gifted friends in the Scottish capital. They founded *The Edinburgh Review*, a learned magazine that concerned itself with literature and politics. For twenty-five years Sydney Smith continued to write pieces for the publication. He used his pen to plead the cause of the oppressed. The horrible slave trade was one of his targets. He fought for the rights of prisoners accused of crimes that carried the death penalty. In those days they were not allowed a defence lawyer. Smith argued that this was a wicked injustice. He also urged that the death penalty for stealing be abolished. He championed the cause of the Catholics,

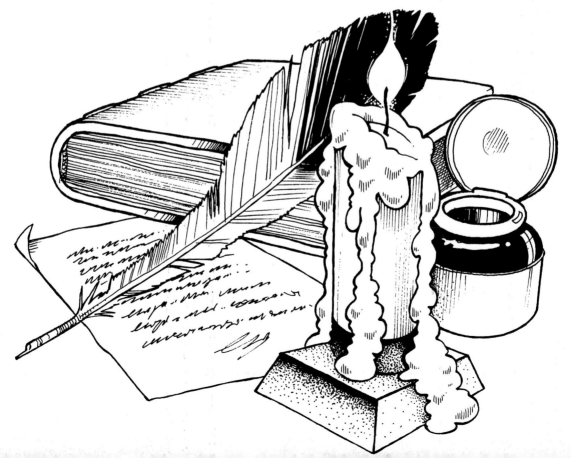

who were barred from many public posts at that time. Smith, who detested religious bigotry, deplored this state of affairs in a series of brilliant articles. They helped to sway public sympathy in favour of the Catholics, who were soon set free by law. He crusaded in print and pulpit for the right of people to elect their members of parliament. His support for the Great Reform Bill, which enlarged the numbers of those entitled to vote, did much to make it the law of the land.

Sydney Smith's fame rang through Europe. The French government, which had recently abolished its monarchy, awarded him a passport in the name of Citizen Smith. But it was as a humorist that he was chiefly celebrated. All accounts agree that he possessed a glittering wit and tireless appetite for fun. More than once he had his listeners literally rolling on the floor in helpless laughter. His attacks on injustice were laced with wild humour and gentle ridicule that made far more impact than long-faced lectures. To his countrymen he proved that a man may laugh and be deadly serious. What a pity that such a wonderful talker lived before the age of radio and television. Only a few of his quips have come down to us, like his remark on a scorching day that '. . . there was nothing for it but to take off my flesh and sit in my bones' and his reply to a doctor who advised him to take a daily walk on an empty stomach: 'Whose?'

Save of the Season

Henri played in goal for Couronne, a village deep in the French countryside. He was quick and brave like most goalkeepers, and practised hard in training sessions to sharpen his skills. For two seasons he stood between the posts, giving a good account of himself in every match. No one doubted that he was the best goalkeeper the village could field.

Then along came Claude Florent, a newcomer to the district. He turned up at the first practice of the season and asked to play in goal. The manager agreed. Henri was placed in one goal and Claude in the other. Anxiously Henri watched to see how the new boy would shape up.

Within half an hour it was clear that Claude was a marvellous 'keeper. He was as fast and graceful as a fish. When the ball struck his gloves it stuck there as if held by a powerful magnet. His courage came close to recklessness. He made three diving fingertip saves that would not have looked out of place in a World Cup match.

Henri watched Claude's display with admiration and despair. He knew at once that he would lose his place to this splendid player. In football the best man gets the job. So he was not surprised when, before the first game of the season, the manager told him he had been dropped. Henri tried to smile but his heart was

heavy. Football meant everything to him and he was very proud of that green woollen jersey.

Soon his spirits returned and he decided to train harder than ever to win back his place. He never missed a practice game. He took up weight-lifting and jogging. By cutting out fatty foods he shed half a stone. But it was all to no purpose. Claude continued to shine between the posts and was never ill or injured. Slowly it became clear to Henri that he would never win back that precious jersey.

One day Henri was walking down the street when he heard a cry of 'Fire!' The shout came from the bottom end of the village, where he saw black smoke billowing from a tall house beside the church. Quickly he ran to the scene. Several people were running here and there in panic. A glance at the house told him that the fire had taken a firm hold, for behind the blackened windows orange flames were leaping wildly. Someone shouted that he had 'phoned for the fire brigade in the nearest town, twenty kilometres away.

At that moment the top window opened and the face of a terrified boy appeared. He was about six years old. 'Save me! Save me!' he screamed. Henri jumped the low garden wall and ran to the front of the house. He looked up at the fear-crazed boy, held up his big hands and yelled: 'Jump!'

The boy's eyes measured the 60-foot drop and 'he shook his head in dumb terror. 'Jump,' commanded Henri. 'It's your only chance.' The boy hesitated for a moment, then clambered out on to the window-ledge. Slowly, legs trembling, he stood up. He looked down at Henri, raised his arms and jumped. His knees struck the goalkeeper square in the chest, but in that instant Henri flung his arms around the child's body. He was hurled to the ground by the force of the boy's fall. But he fell expertly, with all his goalkeeper's skill, cradling the child in his arms. Neither suffered a scratch.

Henri became the village hero, to his great embarrassment. He felt better now about losing his place in the team, for after all he had saved something far more precious than goals – a human life. The priest remarked to the team manager: 'God has his own strange way of using our gifts and making up for our disappointments.'

Francis of Assisi

Pope Innocent III's face wrinkled with distaste as he stared at the man who stood before him. He wore a tattered robe tied at the waist with a length of rope and his hair and beard were shaggy. The pope spoke with cold contempt: 'So you want me to give my blessing to your band of preaching brothers. Well, I'll tell you what to do. Go away and find yourself a pig – you're filthy enough to live in a sty – and preach to him about living a life of poverty like Jesus.'

The man bowed his head and left. He walked straight to the nearest pigsty, lay down and wallowed in the muck. Then, stinking horribly, he went back and asked the pope again to allow him to form a new order of friars. The pope was so impressed that he gave his permission, and the Order of St Francis came into being.

The story is charming but it may not be true. It was told not long after Francis had died. His followers claimed that Francis performed the surprising act to show the pope two of his virtues, obedience and humility.

What cannot be doubted is that Francis was born in the hillside town of Assisi about eight hundred years ago, the son of a rich cloth merchant. He was a happy-go-lucky young man, fond of merry-making but determined to become a great soldier. Then a serious illness struck him down.

For the first time he thought long and hard about his way of living. He promised himself that if he recovered he would live like Jesus. As soon as he was on his feet again he put his plan into action. He gave up his riches and became a wandering preacher, dressed like a tramp. Before long many other young men, moved by his words and sharing his dislike of wealth, joined him in his work of preaching and restoring old churches. Within a few years the followers of Francis were numbered in thousands and had spread over the Christian world.

Francis spent the rest of his days trying to lead a life as close to that of Jesus as possible. At one time he lived in a cave high up on a mountain slope. On the valley floor below stood a cluster of stone houses. Francis often preached to the peasants who lived there. He once tried to describe to them the scene in the stable at Bethlehem. He could see that they found it hard to picture the great event. Then he had an idea. He invited all his listeners up to his cave the next night.

They came, each bearing a burning torch. The column of villagers curved upwards along the rocky paths like a fiery snake. On reaching the cave mouth they stood in silent awe. Inside, in a straw-filled trough, lay a little baby. A man and woman knelt beside him. Shepherds leaned on their staffs, eyes fixed on the new-born child. On the ground lay several cattle, breathing misty plumes into the cold air. Torchlight cast a gentle radiance over the scene. The villagers never forgot it. Francis, they claimed, had staged the first Navitity play, using his friends as actors.

Not long before he died his hands, feet

and body developed the wounds inflicted on Jesus at his crucifixion. Many people since the time of Francis have displayed these marks but his was the first recorded case. Pious folk say they are signs of God's favour, and a few others claim that they are self-inflicted. There are thinkers who tell us that some people love Jesus so deeply that they bring these wounds on themselves by the power of their minds in a way that we cannot yet understand.

One of the favourite stories about Francis is that he preached to the birds. It is certainly true that he loved all animals, calling them his brothers and sisters. His concern for them helped to change men's attitudes. We are a little kinder to dumb creatures than we used to be, believing that they have as much right to the world as we have.

Sister Dora

In 1863 the Walsall Cottage Hospital opened. It was a converted shop and held four beds. Two nurses, members of an Anglican sisterhood, treated an endless stream of patients, many of them child victims of unguarded machines in mines and blast-furnaces. A year later it became necessary to send for a relief nurse. Her name was Sister Dora.

Tall, slim and good-looking, Sister Dora was then aged thirty-three. After a miserable childhood in a Yorkshire rectory she had taught briefly in a village school before joining the Sisters. Her faith in God was deep and strong. It was the kind that spurs to action. She believed that she could best serve God by helping her fellow-men.

Walsall in those days was a grimy, crowded boom-town. By day countless smoking factory chimneys darkened the skies above the huddled slums. At night blast-furnace fires cast a hellish glare on slag-heaps and pools of black water. Like an invisible fog, the smell of tanning leather hung in the air. The people were tough, hard-working and suspicious.

Sister Dora launched herself into her hospital work with a vigour that never flagged. She was an ideal nurse – tireless, self-sacrificing and competent. To her, every patient was a child of God and therefore deserving of loving attention. She slaved from dawn to twilight with a sunny cheerfulness that lit up the little hospital.

At night she visited patients in the fever-ridden slums, fearlessly risking her own life. From the day Sister Dora stepped into the hospital the number of deaths dropped steeply. Gravely injured factory workers pulled through against the odds. People recovered quickly from illnesses that once would have killed them. We shall never know how many survived simply because of their faith in the great-hearted nurse.

Within a short time the people of Walsall revered Sister Dora. Their suspicion and hostility had melted in the face of her labours. Gladly they accepted free treatment. Soon the hospital, now too small to cope with larger numbers and itself a fever hazard, moved to a larger house. Sister Dora was named sister-in-charge. A resident surgeon was appointed. The fame of the hospital spread. Everyone admired its up-to-date medical treatment, its cleanliness, but above all Sister Dora's tender attention to her patients. Fired by her example young women in large numbers eagerly took up nursing. Some were fortunate enough to receive a thorough training from Sister Dora.

Several years before she died a smallpox outbreak struck Walsall. Patients were housed in a new fever hospital. There were no trained nurses. Sister Dora spent six months there, lovingly nursing the sufferers, at grave risk of disfigurement or even death. Simple folk swore she was a saint with miraculous powers, a notion that made her laugh heartily.

Then came the sad day when her doctor told her she had cancer. An operation might – just *might* – save her. Sister Dora refused it. She carried on working without

telling a soul of her illness. But the disease slowly conquered her worn-out body and she died on Christmas Eve, 1878. The people of Walsall raised a marble statue, probably the first to be erected to a British woman not of royal blood.

Christ of the Andes

A chain of steep mountains with peaks like arrow-heads runs the entire length of South America. It is called the Andes. High up on one of the passes stands a giant bronze statue of Jesus. One hand holds a cross and the other is raised in blessing. The statue is known as the Christ of the Andes. How it came to be erected is a story to restore one's faith in men's good sense.

A hundred years ago Chile and Argen-tina, the two countries that lie on each side of the Andes, signed an agreement. It laid down in writing the boundary line be-tween the countries. Sad to say, it was badly worded. Arguments broke out be-tween the two sides. Each country read the agreement differently – in a way that favoured its own claims. Many attempts were made to settle the dispute but all failed. Ill-feeling increased year by year and most people came to believe that war could not be avoided. Both countries made themselves even poorer by raising large armies and gathering huge stocks of weapons. Sensible people cried out warn-ings. When nations stockpile arms, they insisted, those arms are sure to be used. Their words went largely unheard in the

growing clamour. They were branded as traitors and cowards by many of their battle-hungry countrymen.

As the century drew near its end fierce voices, Argentinian and Chilean, cried out for war. Not all these voices belonged to the young soldiers who might be called on to fight. Some older men longed to be young again to take up arms for their country – or so they said. More than one woman declared that she was willing to lay down the lives of her sons and brothers for the Cause.

By good fortune there were powerful forces on the side of peace. The two heads of state, President Errazuriz of Chile and General Roca of Argentina, were of one mind that there should be no war. They invited the Prince of Wales, later King Edward VII, ·and a United States diplomat to sit in judgement on the dispute. Churchmen on both sides of the Andes implored their flocks to remember the words of Jesus: 'Blessed are the peacemakers'.

People came to their senses. The madness of war was averted. When the Prince of Wales and the diplomat handed down their judgements both sides accepted them. Cannons were melted down and fashioned into a statue of Jesus. It stands overlooking the two countries, which have lived at peace ever since.

Lord Shaftesbury

Many years ago a neatly dressed schoolboy was walking along the street when he saw a remarkable sight. A party of men, clearly quite drunk, were staggering along bearing a coffin on their shoulders. They were laughing and singing at the tops of their voices. The boy saw that they were heading towards the churchyard. It was plain that the dead man's friends were too poor to give him a decent funeral. As he watched they fell in a cursing heap on the ground and the coffin clattered to the road. Finally they managed to heave themselves up and set off again on their unsteady journey.

The boy was shocked to see how the poor went to their graves. He could imagine the drunken crew shovelling out a shallow hole in the part of the churchyard set aside for people who died penniless, and covering the coffin with a thin layer of earth, unmarked by a gravestone. After a hasty prayer they would no doubt lurch back to the pub. A life was over. A man had died poor. The soil covered him and there might be nothing to show that he had ever lived.

The boy decided there and then that he would give the rest of his life to helping the poor. He knew it would mean giving up a lot, for he was Lord Ashley, eldest son of the Earl of Shaftesbury. If he wished, he could live a life of ease among the nobility to which he belonged. Or he could become a powerful politician like his father. But the sight of the poor man's funeral drove these grand ideas out of the boy's head. He would use his time on earth to help the miserable millions.

Eleven years later Lord Ashley became a Member of Parliament. He still remembered the vow he had made and was determined to carry it out. He had an early chance to do so when he went to work at the India Board of Control – India at that time being ruled by the British.

Many Indians chose to have their bodies burned after death. Their laws laid down that their widows must burn themselves in the fire that cremated their husbands. The British Government, although it detested this cruel practice, did nothing about it for fear of offending the Indians. Lord Ashley and others spoke up against it and had it stopped.

Next he turned his attention to the lives of the poor of his own country. What he found horrified him. Many workers, including women and young children, spent as many as thirteen hours a day in the cotton mills and down the mines. Boys aged four and five were sent naked up chimneys to clean them. Often they caught cancer of the skin. Thirty thousand home-

less children wandered the streets of London. More than seven families in every ten lived in one room. Children who slaved in factories were often whipped to make them work harder.

Lord Ashley set out to change all this. He spoke out in Parliament, wrote, lectured and argued with anyone who would listen. We must, he repeated, make the lives of the workers, especially those of our women and children, less animal-like. This is a Christian country, he kept saying, and every person is equal in the sight of God and must be treated fairly. We must allow them to lead decent lives, with time to relax and have a few hours' enjoyment every day. We must pass laws which will stop people being used in this heartless manner.

Some agreed with the young man but many did not, especially the factory owners and his fellow noblemen. They told him angrily that the workers must toil for long hours so that the mills could keep going; otherwise profits would fall, the factories would close and the workers lose their jobs. They scolded him for what they saw as his wickedness in unsettling the poor by giving them hope that their lives might become easier.

Lord Ashley was hurt by what his opponents said about him but he never let it stop him from doing what he thought was right. He pressed the government by every means in his power to pass new laws. They refused. He tried again and again. Successive governments, warned by the factory-owners, held out against any change. But by now many people had come to think like Lord Ashley. They had read his

accounts of the dreadful conditions of the poor, and they backed him. Slowly the government gave way and passed laws which improved the working lives of masses of people. Finally children were stopped from working altogether.

Lord Ashley became the Earl of Shaftesbury when his father died and it is by this name that we read of him in the history books. As well as helping the factory workers he made conditions better for patients in mental hospitals. He fought against the slave trade and had some share in stopping it. He persuaded the government and the officials in town halls to build houses for working people.

To sum up, the pink-faced schoolboy who had watched the drunken funeral kept his word. He did spend his life helping others. He never sought power or money. For most of his long life he was in debt, as he gave generously to the poor. When he died thousands of people in factories all over the country decided to show that they appreciated what he had done for them. They gave what small amounts of money they could afford to raise a monument to Lord Shaftesbury. It took the form of the statue of Eros which still stands in Piccadilly Circus in the heart of London.

Mother Maria

Some people are revered for their noble lives, others for a noble death. A rare few are remembered for both. Such a one was Mother Maria.

Her real name was Elizabeth Pilenko. She was born in Russia towards the end of the last century. Although she came of a rich family she threw in her lot with the poor at an early age. In those days the Tsar, the richest king on earth, ruled a land where thousands died of hunger every year. He was a weak but stubborn man who believed that he alone was fit to govern. As time passed, anger against the Tsar grew to fury. When he was swept from his throne in 1917 Elizabeth, like most young Russians, had bright hopes for the future of her country.

Her hopes faded quickly. Under the new rulers conditions became even worse. Famines filled the cemeteries. Uncounted numbers of men and women were put to death or imprisoned. Sickened by her country's plight but helpless to remedy it, Elizabeth resolved to leave Russia for ever.

She arrived in Paris in 1923. Without delay she joined a sisterhood of nuns. Her duties took her to some of the poorest districts in the city. There she visited the old and the sick. She prepared meals, washed dishes and did all the household chores her patients were unable to perform. Moreover, she carried out her work of mercy with a cheerfulness that endeared her to everyone. Some years later she founded a hospital for severely ill patients. She was now known as Mother Maria.

In 1940 German soldiers, who had quickly crushed the French armies, entered Paris. One of their first acts was to round up as many Jews as they could lay their hands on. These unfortunates were crammed in special trains – some of which had been used to transport cattle – and moved out of the city. Mother Maria hid hundreds of Jews in her hospital and helped them to escape to safety. Then one day the German State Police arrested her and she was sent to a concentration camp at Ravensbruck.

The camp housed huge numbers of Jews. They were given barely enough food to keep them alive. Later it was decided to kill them all. They were put to death by shooting and hanging, and buried in mass graves. Eventually, in order to save time and bullets, the Germans began to use gas chambers. These were large rooms in which squads of prisoners could be killed quickly by poison gas. The guards pretended they were shower-rooms so that their victims would enter willingly.

Mother Maria did everything in her power to help her fellow-prisoners. She shared her last crust, nursed the sick and comforted the dying. Starvation soon reduced her to skin and bone but did not sap her sunny spirit. Even the guards called her 'that wonderful Russian nun'.

One day a batch of women were assembled outside the 'shower-room' for execution. A young girl, guessing the true purpose of the chamber, began to scream in terror. Mother Maria ran forward. 'Don't be frightened,' she said. 'I'll come with you.' Murmuring words of comfort to the stricken girl she shuffled towards the gas chamber.

Why Christians Join Their Hands

Do you know why we join our hands when we pray? Perhaps you think – as many people do – that we are picturing a church steeple. Well, this is not so; men joined their hands long before there were any steeples.

No one is quite certain when the custom began but it must have been fairly soon after men first raised armies and took prisoners in battle. These captives had their wrists tied together, hands pointing upwards, and were led back to the victors' camp. At some later time the joining of hands came to stand for a gesture of surrender. If a wounded or frightened warrior wished to be taken prisoner he joined his hands.

As time went on the act was used by anyone who wished to show that he was less worthy than another. Many Indians began to join their hands at prayer to show how weak they were in the presence of their God. To this day Indians do it as a form of greeting. By joining their hands they are saying, in effect, 'See, I am in your power. My hands cannot take up a weapon to harm you.'

Some time before the birth of Jesus the Greeks and Romans took up the joining of hands in their religious services. By doing

it they were asking their gods to tie the hands of the evil spirits and prevent them from harming mankind.

Now the early Christians at prayer stood with outstretched arms, like the Hebrews from whom they had taken over many old practices. Some say that this dramatic stance showed a young, fighting religion, eager to embrace the whole world. Later, when this had come about, Christians crossed their arms on their breasts when they prayed. This is said to indicate a quieter, humbler attitude. Finally, about eleven hundred years ago, Christians began to join their hands in prayer.

There were probably several reasons for this. They may have borrowed the custom from the great lords of the time, who made their men join hands as a sign that they would serve their masters faithfully. Probably the Indians influenced the change for, as we have learned, the Hindus prayed with joined hands from early times. It is possible that many Christians felt that a gentle gesture while praying was more suitable for a religion of love. No doubt someone pointed out that when the hands are joined they cannot fidget and distract the worshipper from his prayers.

For any or all of these reasons, Christians began to join their hands. So when you do this you are saying to your God, 'I am yours, bound to you as were the prisoners of old to their captors. Do with me as you wish.'

Harriet Tubman

At a word from their leader the straggling line of Negroes sank to the ground for a well-deserved rest. They had struggled across rivers, mountains and forests, travelling always by night. All were exhausted. Gratefully they sprawled on the verges of the hillside that led north to freedom. Only their leader – a stocky, muscular figure – remained standing, revolver in hand, eyes scanning the high road below for the pursuing slave-masters.

'I can't go on,' sobbed a young man, his voice faint with fatigue. 'My feet are bleeding. Let's all go back. If they catch us they'll —'

'We're going on.' The words were hissed by the leader. 'We're going on to freedom. You can't go back now. The slaveholders would force you to tell them our route to the North. I'd blow your head off first, as sure as my name's Harriet Tubman.'

Yes, their leader was a woman. She had grown up as a slave on the cotton and rice farms of Maryland. The life was harsh but she grew strong and active in the open air. Later she was taken into the farmer's house as a kitchen-maid. Her mistress often beat her with a rawhide whip for small mistakes like breaking a cup. There was nothing she could do about it. Like most blacks in that part of the United States she was 'owned' by her master.

Harriet could not read or write. There were no schools for black children. But her wits were sharp and she needed no books to teach her what an unjust world she lived in. She knew that in other parts of the country her people were free and prosperous.

When the master died Harriet feared that she would be sold to an even worse slave-owner. She ran away to Pennsylvania, one of the Northern states where slavery was illegal. There she began to earn her living as a cook in hotels and private homes. She delighted in being a free woman and grieved for the family and friends she had left behind. Harriet decided to help her people escape.

She secretly slipped back into Maryland, visited a number of Negroes who wished to be free and led a party of them back to Pennsylvania. Pleased with her success, she repeated the journey. Once again she guided a band of slaves to a new and better life. In the years that followed she made nineteen such raids and freed about three hundred people. These included her mother and father, for whom she bought a cottage with her savings, and several brothers and sisters. Naturally the slaveholders were furious at losing their Negroes through Harriet's 'underground railway', as it came to be known, and some say they offered a large reward for her capture. Many times they came close to catching her. When danger was near Harriet knelt down and prayed to God, for her faith was deep and trusting.

When she was about forty years old civil war broke out between those states that wished to do away with slavery and those that insisted on keeping it. Harriet enlisted as a nurse with the Northern army. More than once she made the perilous journey to the South, where she gathered valuable information behind enemy lines. No one was more joyful than Harriet when the slave states were defeated and all Negroes were freed.

In her later years Harriet Tubman's story became widely known. Writers praised her deeds in glowing pages. Statesmen spoke in her honour. Queen Victoria presented her with a medal. None of these high compliments, however, made her prouder than the title 'the Moses of her people'.

Dietrich Bonhoeffer

In December 1941, Hitler, disappointed by the progress of his invasion of Russia, dismissed Field-Marshal von Brauchitsch and assumed the post of commander-in-chief. This was a bitter blow to a group of highly-placed Germans who had been plotting to overthrow Hitler with the aid of Brauchitsch. For one member of the resistance network, Dietrich Bonhoeffer, a Christian minister, the news brought about a crucial decision.

At the age of thirty-five Bonhoeffer had won wide fame for his religious writings. He was admired for his tireless efforts to unite the divided Church. Before the war he had struggled endlessly but unsuccessfully to prevent the Nazis from dominating the Lutheran Church. In 1940 he joined the Military Intelligence Department. This enabled him to travel to neutral countries for the official purpose of spreading German propaganda among fellow priests. Secretly he informed them of the plan to remove Hitler and sue for peace. He persuaded his old friend George Bell, Bishop of Chichester, to seek the help of the British and American governments for the conspirators. Bell met with no success.

To Bonhoeffer the dismissal of Brauchitsch left open only one course of action – assassination. He declared himself willing to perform the act with his own hand. The decision must have cost profound grief to such a devout Christian. Plans were set in motion to kill Hitler. The task was daunting, for the dictator was guarded with fanatical devotion.

In March 1943 two assassination attempts were made. In the first a time-bomb failed to explode. The second misfired due to Hitler's cutting short a visit to an arsenal. A fortnight later Bonhoeffer, his brother-in-law Hans von Dohnanyi, who had provided the bomb, and a third plotter were arrested.

So began two years of imprisonment. Bonhoeffer used them to write some of his most important works. He read widely and kept himself fit by daily exercise. His cheerful kindliness comforted the other prisoners. Even the warders – some of them brutal ruffians – were so impressed by his behaviour that they sought his advice on their personal problems.

At the beginning of April 1945 Hitler was shown the recently discovered diary of Admiral Canaris, head of the Military Intelligence Department. It revealed not only Canaris' own involvement in the conspiracy but the names of his comrades, including Bonhoeffer. The furious dictator ordered their immediate execution. When Bonhoeffer learned of the death sentence he calmly remarked that his earthly life was at an end but his eternal life was just beginning. At dawn on a grey morning he was hanged and his body burned. A month later Germany surrendered.

The Heroic Village

One day the village tailor received a bale of cloth from London. It felt damp so he hung it in front of the fire to dry out. Within a few days he was dead. 'The plague!' cried the neighbours, crossing themselves with trembling fingers. 'It's come with the cloth. Thousands are dying in London. Now it's here in Eyam.'

'What's the plague, dad?' asked a small boy.

'It's a deadly disease,' was the answer. 'It spreads quickly from one person to another – we're not sure how. One day you begin to cough, shiver and sneeze. A blotchy stain shows on your chest. Next you're in bed with a high fever. Then you have little chance of getting better.'

Before the end of that month – September 1665 – five more people died. Fear gripped the Derbyshire village. The wife of the priest, William Mompesson, urged him to leave the place, taking her and their two children. Sadly he said no. His duty lay in Eyam with his flock. She should take the children to safety with her family in Yorkshire. She bravely refused to leave him but sent the boy and girl away until the plague had run its course.

In October twenty-three villagers died. November brought seven deaths and December nine. The frosts of winter had halted the spread of the disease. Everyone

Food would be collected at several points around the village and paid for by placing money in stone troughs full of water with vinegar added. It was believed that this made the coins safe to handle.

So the brave country folk suffered on. Many terrified householders left their homes and went to live in makeshift huts a little way outside the village. Still the plague killed nineteen in June and fifty-six in July. Eyam was quite cut off from the world – or not quite, for one man broke the rule that no one should go in or out. He was young Rowland Torre, whose home was a few miles from Eyam. His girl-friend Emmot Siddal lived in the village. Her father, brother and four sisters had died of the plague. In spite of her warnings of the risk he was running the young man insisted on meeting her at the boundary to comfort her and talk of the happy day in August when they would be married. One day Rowland turned up but Emmot did not. She had died.

All through that terrible summer William Mompesson went from house to house, bringing comfort and medicine to the dying. In August his wife died. In October the number of dead fell to fourteen. Hope ran high. Was it over? On 1st November the last victim of the plague was buried. The villagers burned furniture and bedding lest it might house the invisible killer. Two hundred and sixty people had gone to their graves. Only two had run away. One of these was Emmot's mother, the last of her family, half-crazed with loneliness and sorrow. The brave men and women of Eyam had shown the world how and when to risk their lives.

hoped with all their hearts that the terror was finished. When Spring came the frightful illness struck again and again until every home in Eyam was a house of mourning.

William Mompesson spoke to a crowded church. He told them that a full-scale plague was raging. They must stay in the village until it was over. To run away meant bringing it to other places and other people. Staying at home placed them in greater danger but it was the right thing to do. The villagers nodded in agreement, their faces pale with dread. Mompesson said that he would no longer preach in the church, for large meetings spread the killer, but in a roomy cave out in the open.

Wilhelm Rontgen

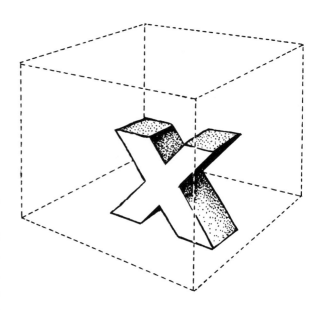

In the darkened room the professor trembled with excitement. Before him stood a cone-shaped glass tube carefully wrapped in black cardboard. An electromagnetic current throbbed through the tube. On a nearby cardboard screen a faint green light flickered. That light, he knew, was caused by invisible rays from the tube – rays powerful enough to pierce the black paper. They were rays unknown to science.

That day – 8 November 1895 – was an important one for the whole human race. The professor, Wilhelm Rontgen, saw at once how vital his discovery would be in many fields, especially medicine. It would now be possible for doctors to look into a living body, with all the benefits that would bring. Bullets could be located and bone damage judged at a glance. Early detection of disease would lead to better chances of recovery.

Rontgen let the world know of his miracle rays without the least delay. He was sharply aware that their immediate use would save lives. He could have become rich by selling his knowledge but he wished to make his discovery freely available to all at the earliest moment. He called his rays X-rays. He did so because in algebra the letter X denotes an unknown quantity.

Experts everywhere hailed Rontgen's work as a giant advance. Scientists in many lands began to study this new area of knowledge. They found that X-rays could be used for all sorts of purposes, from observing the structure of tiny particles of matter to exposing fake paintings. They proved to be extremely useful in industry. X-rays can pin-point the flaws in wood and metal. They help the expert to cut precious stones – an intricate task that needs all possible aids.

Rontgen's name and fame rang round the world. Wealth and titles were offered to him but he refused them, for he was a truly modest man. He did accept the Nobel prize for physics. His last years were made miserable by lack of money.

An interesting fact about Wilhelm Rontgen is that he was expelled from school for misbehaviour and failed to get into college at his first attempt. So it is not always the sober swots who reach the greatest heights.

Woodbine Willie (1883–1929)

The troop-train was packed with helmeted British soldiers, ready to set off for the Front. The place was Rouen, the year 1916. Sergeants, checklists in hand, bawled last-minute orders. The engine gave a long preparatory hiss. A lone figure on the platform walked the whole length of the train, pausing at every carriage. Across each of his shoulders hung a bulging knapsack. One held packets of cigarettes and the other copies of the New Testament. He handed a book and a packet to every soldier, with a few words of encouragement for all.

'Who's the funny-looking geezer, sarge?' asked a teenage squaddie.

'Don't you know, son?' came the reply. 'That's Woodbine Willie.'

His real name was Geoffrey Studdert Kennedy. He was born and brought up in his father's vicarage in a poor district of Leeds. He was educated at Leeds Grammar School and Trinity College, Dublin. After several years as a schoolmaster he felt the call to the priesthood. He entered Ripon Clergy College and was ordained in 1910. He spent his early years as a clergyman in Rugby, Leeds and Worcester.

Studdert Kennedy soon showed his deep love of the poor. He threw all his remarkable energy into helping them. His help extended far beyond their religious problems. In the harsh struggle for jobs, homes and decent living conditions he was always at hand with practical aid. He gave most of his salary away. His concern for the poor was not that of a dutiful Christian carrying out a painful obligation. Quite simply, he was happiest among down-and-outs.

He became well known as a fascinating preacher. His sermons, which he took great pains to prepare, revealed his wide learning and deep sincerity. They also displayed the clownish side of his nature. Sometimes he would sit on the edge of the pulpit, legs dangling, and set his listeners giggling at a string of jokes and droll remarks. Soon there was a demand for Studdert Kennedy to speak at open-air meetings.

It was a time of widespread change. Working people, banded together in strong trade unions, were demanding better lives. Many of them had come to see the Church as one of the forces ranged against them. Its close links with the ruling classes drew increasingly bitter attacks. Its teaching that we should seek happiness only in the next life seemed a stumbling-block to progress in this one. A better educated public was reading books that struck at the basic beliefs of Christianity. In public halls and at street corners speakers poured scorn on the old order. People deserted the Church in large numbers.

Studdert Kennedy shared many of these new views. Indeed, he was rejected by many of his fellow-priests as 'that Socialist parson'. But he firmly believed that the central truths of the Christian faith must not be abandoned: he saw that there was a real danger of throwing the baby out with the bath water. He launched himself into the noisy world of public speaking. From platforms and soap-boxes he trumpeted the Church's age-old message. He drew packed meetings with his blend of fiery argument and knockabout fun.

When the First World War broke out in 1914 Kennedy saw it as a clear-cut struggle between good and evil. He advised every fit young man to fight. A year later he became an army chaplain. He did not confine his duties to holding services and delivering pious sermons. He ate, drank and sang with his soldiers. He wrote their letters and procured little luxuries for them. It was his habit of distributing cigarettes that earned him the nickname Woodbine Willie.

In the summer of 1916 Kennedy was posted to the Front. He insisted on sharing the dangers of the forward trenches within range of enemy guns. For his bravery in attending the wounded while under heavy fire he was awarded the Military Cross. Suddenly he was famous. The newspapers, eager to print something less heartbreaking than their long lists of dead, joyously hailed their hero padre.

The hero padre took no pleasure in his fame. He had grown bitter in the mud and blood of the trenches. The appalling waste of lives tormented him. In a number of verses written in the everyday accents of the fighting soldier he exposed the terrible nature of war.

With the coming of peace Studdert Ken-

nedy took up the post of chief missioner of the Industrial Christian Fellowship. This was a body whose purpose was to revive the Christian faith among working people. Despite continuous bad health – he had suffered from asthma from an early age – Kennedy embarked on a punishing round of speeches and lecture tours. In several books he explained the primary beliefs of Christianity and deplored the spirit of greed he found everywhere. In March 1929, while on a speaking engagement in Liverpool, he collapsed and died. When they carried out his body for removal to Worcester an unknown man – an ex-soldier, some say – stepped forward and placed a packet of Woodbines on the coffin.

Kick

Stephen and Kick were friends. 'Kick' was a nickname. The boy's real name was Kenneth but he had such a dreadful stammer that when anyone asked him his name he answered, 'Kick, Kick, Kick, Kenneth.' So the boys at the boarding-school called him Kick. No one played with the stuttering boy and Stephen had felt sorry for him. He made friends with Kick and the two were always together.

From the beginning Stephen liked the school. He was clever and good at games, which meant that he got on well with both masters and boys. Kick, on the other hand, was miserable. His stammer made some of the crueller boys laugh and he never got used to being hurt. He found school work very hard, for he was not nearly as bright as his friend. As the first year drew to an end Stephen often wondered what was to become of Kick, who was becoming more and more moody and worried about falling behind in his lessons.

After the summer holidays Kick did not come back. He wrote to Stephen saying that the headmaster had told his father that the school work was too difficult for his son and that he would be happier at a different type of school. Stephen was sorry. He had really liked Kick. But soon the memory of his friend faded from his mind as he threw himself into the hurly-burly of school life.

The years passed. Stephen, now a young scientist, was playing in a tennis tournament in a strange town. Between games he felt hungry and decided to have a meal. He asked where the best restaurant in town was and was directed to a glassy new building. On entering he was struck by the stylish look of the room and its snowy tablecloths. He sat down, ordered a meal and looked around.

In a corner a group of waiters were hovering attentively around a young man. Must be somebody important, thought Stephen. Then the man turned his head and he saw that it was Kick. Kick saw him at the same moment and a broad smile lit his face. He rose and came over to Stephen's table. 'Stephen,' he said, shaking hands warmly.

'Kick,' answered Stephen.

The other laughed. 'I haven't been called that for ages,' he said. He sat down and the two young men began to talk. Stephen learned to his surprise that Kick owned the restaurant. He was further surprised to note that Kick's stammer had completely disappeared. He was, it seemed to Stephen, a highly intelligent and pleasant man. 'How did you come to own this posh place?' he asked.

Kick shrugged his shoulders. 'Luck, I suppose.'

They chatted for an hour and then Stephen had to hurry back to the tennis courts. They promised to write to each other and keep in touch.

After the tournament Stephen got into conversation with a local man and happened to mention Kick's name. The man knew him well and told Stephen the full story of Kick's life since he had left the boarding-school.

His father had made him a pot-boy in the family pub. He spent long hours washing and carrying bottles. Most of his work was in the cellars and he had little time for the usual pastimes of teenage boys. At sixteen he began to serve behind the counter and his father, who was a lazy man and too fond of the contents of his bottles, gave up working altogether and left the running of the pub to Kick. This was a mighty load for a boy of his age but Kick buckled down to the job manfully.

Suddenly his father died of a heart attack. Kick found himself the breadwinner for his mother and two little sisters. Worse was to follow. They discovered that the father had been up to his ears in debt. The pub had to be sold to pay up. Kick was out of a job and the family was forced to live in a three-roomed flat.

He became a counter assistant in a cafe. The money was poor – just enough to keep his family eating. Kick spent as little as he possibly could on himself. In the evenings he went to cookery lessons, for he had already decided to go into the restaurant business. At week-ends he took a part-time job as a waiter in an hotel.

At the age of nineteen Kick opened his own small cafe in the High Street. He slaved from dawn to sunset to make it a success. The cafe made enough money to provide his sisters with a good education and his mother with a comfortable home. Five years later he had done so well that he was able to open the finest restaurant in town. Everywhere he was spoken of as a young man of real worth.

As he motored home that evening Stephen mused, 'All these years I've thought that Kick was one of those people who seem bound to make a mess of their lives. It just shows how badly we can misjudge others, and how much can be done by sheer determination.'

Marinus, Martyr

Two hundred years after the death of Jesus the Romans still ruled Palestine. The Tenth Legion was stationed in Caesarea, where the Christian faith had flourished since Paul was imprisoned there. One of the officers was a man named Marinus. He came from a well-connected and wealthy family. A serious and able man, he had moved swiftly up the ladder of command.

The post of colonel fell vacant. Marinus seemed the best choice to fill the position. No one was surprised when the order for his appointment came through. His brother-officers were pleased – all except one. This man was bitter, for he believed that he was best fitted to fill the vacancy. He rushed to the city magistrate, Achaeus by name, and declared that Marinus was a Christian. Achaeus summoned Marinus and asked if it was true. Proudly the soldier affirmed that he was indeed a follower of Jesus.

The magistrate heard the news with mixed feelings. How could a Roman officer give up a successful career for his invisible God? He explained to Marinus that his offence was punishable by death. The choice before him was simple. He could return to the long-standing faith of his forefathers. By doing so he would be free to continue his fine career, and the highest posts in the Roman Empire would not be beyond his grasp. Or he could cling on to this Christian nonsense and perish. Would he now come to his senses, give up this strange new faith and sacrifice to the emperors? Marinus firmly refused. Achaeus, still desiring to save the soldier, adjourned the hearing for three hours to give him a chance to change his mind.

Outside the courthouse Marinus was drawn aside by Theotecnus, bishop of Caesarea. He took him to the church and placed him before the altar. Then, picking up the book of the scriptures, the bishop said, 'You must choose between this, and that,' pointing to the sword at Marinus' side. No further words were needed. Without speaking the soldier reached out and took the book.

Three hours later the court was recalled. Achaeus asked the prisoner if he still clung to his Christian beliefs. Marinus asserted that he would remain a Christian until his life's end, however near that end might be. The magistrate unwillingly passed sentence and Marinus was taken out and put to death.

Mary Slessor

There are some people whose lives blaze with energy and achievement. The writer who sets out to tell their story in a small space can despair of the size of his task. Perhaps his best plan is to present his facts in short phrases, like a student's lecture notes.

Name: Mary Slessor. Born 2 December 1848, Aberdeen. Father shoemaker, mother weaver. Family moved to Dundee. Mary started work (half-days) in textile mill aged eleven. Rest of half-days in school learning 3 R's. Deeply religious. Admired Livingstone. Resolved to go to Africa as missionary.

Landed Calabar, 1876. Area known as White Man's Grave. Calabar a port at mouth of Cross river. White traders collected palm oil in exchange for European goods including guns, gin, rum. Mary began teaching at mission house. Learned tribal language. Spent much time among African women, preaching Christianity. Often ill - malaria.

Home on holiday, 1879. On return to Calabar sent to village three miles up-river. Became its preacher, doctor, teacher, instructor in home improvement. Explored rain forests inhabited by snakes, leopards, etc. Saved baby girl twin abandoned in bush by parents. Africans believed twins cursed. Custom was to kill babies and banish mother. Named her Janie and brought her up along with many other abandoned babies.

Mary sent home ill, 1883. Recovered, went on lecture tour. Gained large amount of money and many recruits for missions. Returned to Africa. Moved up-river to Ekenge, village peopled by savage tribes. Persuaded chiefs to build mission houses in Ekenge and nearby village. Found that tribes were dying out through fighting and drinking. When chief died witchcraft always suspected. Poisoned drink then forced on his wives, relatives, slaves. If they vomited and recovered, innocent. If died, guilty. Most died. Mary opposed this custom in face of drunken, armed tribes-men. Saved many lives. Made vice-consul with power to try offenders.

1904. Though failing in health moved inland to Itu with seven children. Hospital built there. Spent much time judging legal squabbles. Known and revered as 'the white ma'. Campaigned without cease against twin-murder and ordeal by poison. Saw first churches built in area.

September 1914. Struck down by fever and dysentery. Died 13 January 1915. Buried at Calabar in cemetery overlooking port where she had docked forty years earlier.

Socrates

Long before the time of Jesus a boy named Socrates was born near the city of Athens. Nobody knows very much about the early part of his life but some think he was a sculptor, or carver in stone, when he was a young man. He was certainly a soldier for a time and fought for Athens against other cities. He was big, tough and ugly.

From his youth until his death at a good age Socrates lived in Athens. He spent his life as a teacher. He was not a teacher of the kind we have today, that is, a person who helps children to learn in special buildings. For a start, there were no schools as we know them in old Greece. Secondly, Socrates set out to teach adults, not children.

What did he teach? He taught his students to think clearly and to live well. Socrates believed that we all have a great deal of true knowledge in our minds that we don't even know about. Because we are lazy we do not use our brains to arrange this information in its correct order, which would help us to understand ourselves and how we can lead good lives. Socrates often showed how confused our ideas can be by gently questioning his friends. He made them see that many of their notions con-tradicted each other. He proved that what seemed the clearest common sense to them could be knocked flat by a clever man like himself.

He was the first to teach that the most important thing for man to study is him-

self. The Greeks of his time had made great strides in finding out about the world around them but most of their ideas about themselves were the sort of tangled beliefs, not supported by hard thinking, that Socrates spoke most strongly against. He insisted that our ideas must be built on facts supported by clear reasoning.

Many Athenians came to admire the great man for his wise teachings and to love him for his kindness. He spent all his time teaching in the market-place, in his friends' houses or wherever he happened to come to rest. He never looked for power or money. He led a life of cheerful poverty.

Now, men who lead good lives always make many enemies. When they are clever as well as good the rage of those who hate them rises to boiling point. So it was with Socrates. His enemies put him on trial for – they said – filling the heads of young people with wicked ideas about the gods. The wise old man made a fine speech in his own defence but it was useless. He was sentenced to die thirty days later. It would have been easy for him to escape from prison. He had many friends, some of whom urged him to do so. They told him that most of the citizens of Athens were shocked to hear of his death sentence. If he did go free no one would try too hard to recapture him.

Socrates refused to escape. He had always taught that the laws should be obeyed, and even though his own death was plainly unfair he preferred to be killed in order to give a good example to others. He spent his last month in prison talking calmly with his friends as if nothing had happened or was going to happen. On the evening marked out for his death Socrates cheerfully discussed whether we live on after death, which he believed.

At last the jailer brought in the cup of poison. The old man made a little joke and, putting the cup to his mouth, quickly drank the deadly liquid. Some of his friends sobbed. He scolded them gently. Then he lay down and in a short time he died.

Some say that Socrates was the wisest man who ever lived, and it is not difficult to back up that claim. But whether it is true or not no one can deny that he lived a wonderful life and died a splendid death.

Father Borrelli

Fatty, the leader of the street gang, strutted over to the ragged stranger and demanded: 'Who are you?' At the same time he jerked the peak of the young man's cap, bringing him instantly to his feet. The stranger, torn suddenly from the warmth of the pavement grating over a baker's oven, stared into Fatty's threatening eyes. Then he spat in his face. The teenage gang boss quivered with rage. The other man thrust his hand in his jacket pocket in a gesture everyone understood. With the other hand he grasped the leader's arm and demanded: 'What's the matter with you? I've got a right to a bit of warmth, haven't I, same as anyone else? And something to eat too, and who's stopping me?'

To the astonishment of the gang Fatty did not hit back. Grinning ruefully he took a razor-blade from his pocket. He handed it to the newcomer with the remark that if he had not managed to get his hand into his pocket first he would have been slashed so badly that his own mother would not have recognized him. From that moment the tattered stranger was a member of the gang.

What Fatty did not know was that the newcomer's pocket was empty. And he would have been dumbfounded if the man had told him who he was. His name was Mario Borrelli and he was a Catholic priest.

Father Borrelli was ordained shortly after the end of the Second World War.

Italy had suffered terribly in the fighting. In his native city of Naples every kind of criminal racket flourished amid poverty and squalor. Gangs of homeless boys, some as young as eight, roamed the streets. These urchins slept rough and managed to stay alive by thieving, begging and other low-life tricks. A favourite dodge was to gather hundreds of cigarette-butts, take out the tobacco and sell it in the market.

Father Borrelli, who had taken up a teaching appointment, longed to help the street boys. He knew he could not do so as a priest, for the urchins hated all persons in authority. Then he had a bright idea: if you can't meet 'em, join 'em. Removing his dog-collar, he donned tatty old clothes, slouched along to Fatty's gang and sat down beside them. When Fatty demanded to know his name he refused to answer, for he had decided to keep his identity a secret. And just to prove that he too was tough, he spat in the gang leader's face.

From that day the priest led a double life. During the day he was a respectable teacher. When darkness fell he became a shabby vagabond drifting through the alleys of Naples, sleeping on the pavements like the rest of the gang. They nicknamed him Crooked Nose and came to trust him completely. By sharing their hardships and dangers – he had to take a few beatings – he learned to understand them. Meanwhile he was making secret preparations to help them.

Father Borrelli got permission to use a derelict church. He whitewashed the walls, installed electric light, laid straw mattresses on the floor and set out wooden boxes as tables. Then, through church friends, he let the street gangs know that there was a place where they could eat and sleep.

At first they came in ones and twos, suspicious of Father Borrelli's priest friends who gave them a simple meal and a blanket and mattress for the night. Later the numbers grew. The youngsters were encouraged to collect and sell scrap-iron to provide furniture for their home. Very soon they were running the house themselves.

Naturally Father Borrelli's secret had to leak out some time. One night when he was in the home, dressed in his night-time rags, an urchin recognized his picture in a newspaper. He at once told the others. To the priest's amazement and delight they crowded around him hugging him and clinging to his hands. Those tough little backstreet hooligans knew what he had done for them and were determined to show him that they appreciated it.

The Beaver

Do you know which animal is most like man, not in appearance but in way of living? Some say the dolphin, some the ant. There are good arguments for both. The dolphin, say its supporters, is nearest in intelligence to man. The ant, say others, lives like us in large groups, with each member given his own special task. Others vote for the beaver.

You must have seen a picture of a beaver. He is a large, furry animal with a flattened tail and two big front teeth. A really big one can weigh as much as a ten-year-old child. He has sharp claws and long brown hair.

When the beaver is two years old his mother turns him out of the home to make a new life for himself. This is not an act of cruelty, for if every beaver were allowed to stay in the lake in which he was born it would soon become overcrowded. He sets off overland to find a stream. On the way he often teams up with a female who has also been turned away from home and they carry on their search together.

Having found a stream they set to work. Swiftly they cut down trees with their strong teeth. They use the bark as food. The rest of the tree is cut into smaller lengths which they drag or carry to the stream. These stakes are fixed into the bed of the moving water, pointing against the current. Smaller branches are fitted between the stakes. Then the beavers dig up mud and stones from the bottom and cement the whole barrier together. This is called a dam.

Soon the stream, prevented from flowing along its natural path, spreads out and forms a small lake. This is exactly what the beaver wants. He needs an expanse of water in which he can swim, safe from enemies such as the wolf and man. But his work is not finished. His dam is being continually pressed by a growing mass of water which will, if nothing is done, overflow and wreck it. So the beaver and his mate work non-stop to strengthen their dam.

His home is called a lodge. It is made from thick branches and young trees built up above the surface of the water, often on a small island. It is so strongly put together that not even a bear can pull it apart. Inside this firm web of branches is a platform where the beaver can feed and sleep.

Baby beavers are born, usually three or four at a time, in April or May. For a month they stay in the lodge. Then their mother takes them out into the lake and teaches them to swim, anxiously holding their tails in her mouth. When they are two years old and fully grown she chases them off to find a home for themselves, as she herself had been pushed out by her mother.

The beaver works with brisk energy. Like man, he can change the shape of the countryside with his dams. Indeed, it is possible that our cave-men ancestors learned to build dams by watching the beaver. This fine creature harms no other animal; on the contrary, the lakes that he creates provide watering-places for many a thirsty beast. We can learn a lot from the beaver about how to help ourselves and others.

Dr Aggrey

'You can play a tune of sorts on the white piano keys. You can also play some kind of tune on the black notes. But for real music, rich in harmony, you must use both the white and the black notes.' So said Dr Aggrey, the black African thinker. He was speaking of the ties between blacks and whites in Africa. They must work peacefully together, he urged, and pass on to their children all that is best in the cultures of Europe and Africa. Although he never said so, he himself was a fine example of the type of African he hoped to produce.

Kodwo Aggrey, his father's seventeenth child, was born in Ghana just over a hundred years ago. He attended a Methodist school where he was baptized and took the name James. His Christian faith grew deep and strong. At fifteen he became a teacher. His salary was four pounds a year, for which he taught village children all week and took Sunday school. At sixteen he returned to teach in his home town, Cape Coast. His evenings were spent studying science, Greek, Latin and religion. In his early twenties he became a headmaster, a post he soon gave up to sail for the United States. It was to be more than twenty years before he saw Africa again.

He studied at Livingstone College, a Methodist institution in North Carolina, and took up a post there after graduating. He met and married a girl named Rosebud. In addition to his college duties – he taught English, economics and Greek – he became pastor of two village churches. His flock were black and poor. Many were farmers who scratched a hand-to-mouth living on tiny patches of land. Dr Aggrey showed them how to improve their crops by using modern methods and the latest tools.

But it was as a speaker that his fame spread. Crowds filled lecture halls and churches to listen to him. They were impressed by the range of his well-stocked mind, gripped by his power and entertained by his parables and jokes.

In 1920 a commission was set up to examine African education. It was felt that the party should include at least one black man. Dr Aggrey was chosen, 'just to add a touch of colour to the proceedings', as he put it. He returned to Africa where he was greeted everywhere by rapturous crowds. He spoke to them of the black man's dream of governing his own continent, warning them of the need to share responsibility with the whites. His views drove some people to fury. Most whites swore that they would never concede power to the blacks. Many blacks insisted that the white man must leave Africa, condemning Dr Aggrey as a puppet who had been bribed by empty honours. He withstood these attacks with good humour, confident that sensible folk of both colours shared his position.

After a year he returned to the United State. He was now regarded as a leading spokesman for his race. He lectured all over the country. One of Dr Aggrey's main targets was the belief that one race is better than another. This was a piece of wishful thinking, he argued, used by people to enable them to think more highly of themselves.

In 1927 Dr Aggrey returned to Africa. Soon he was busy preparing for the opening of a large new school of which he was to be a vice-principal. In the summer he went home on leave to the United States. He suddenly collapsed and died. Black Africans mourned the loss of a friend who had spoken up for their cause, not in the accents of hate but with the Christian's passion for human brotherhood.

Elizabeth Fry

Try to picture what life in prison was like one hundred and fifty years ago. Imagine, for example, what you would have seen in the women's section of Newgate Prison in London. Most of the inmates were crammed together in one big room. They were dressed in their own filthy rags. Around them ran their children, equally tattered and underfed. Some women were singing, drunk on the gin their friends had smuggled in. Others quarrelled in shrill voices. Some lay without hope on tiny iron beds. Those who had no bed sprawled on wisps of straw or the bare floor. The smell of the place was sickening and its air of despairing misery sent visitors away determined never to set foot in the building again.

On one visitor it had exactly the opposite effect. Her first sight convinced her that she must return to help the sad wretches. Her name was Elizabeth Fry.

She was a wealthy lady who had come from Norwich to live near London. She had done much good work among the poor and sick. An American friend had pressed her to go and see the appalling conditions at Newgate.

On her next visit Elizabeth Fry said she would go into the large cell to talk to the prisoners. The warder begged her not to, warning that it was too dangerous. Elizabeth only smiled and entered. The first thing she did was pick up a ragged child and say, 'Friends, many of you are mothers. I too am a mother. I am distressed for your children. Is there not something we can do for these innocent little ones? Do you want them to grow up to become real prisoners themselves? Are they to learn to be thieves and worse?'

There was silence. The women were touched. A chair was brought for the well-dressed lady. Then they crowded gently around Elizabeth and pleaded with her to help them to mend their broken lives. She promised to do everything in her power and that she would come back often.

She kept her word. She returned and with the help of friends set up a school in the prison. They gave lessons in needlework, knitting, reading and writing. At first the prison governors frowned on this, for they thought the women would soon tire of learning, but to their surprise and pleasure the lessons were a great success. Prisoners grew more interested in life outside and more determined to mend their ways when they were set free. The skills they learned in prison, together with the daily Bible lessons started by Elizabeth, gave them reason to hope that they were not as worthless as they had come to believe.

Elizabeth Fry spent the rest of her life easing the lives of prisoners. She toured the country seeing at first hand the treatment of people in jail. She wrote a report on what she saw and sent it to the government. She let members of the House of Commons know exactly what she wanted to see them do – create separate prisons for women run by women warders, introduce useful jobs for prisoners, do away with the punishment of keeping an inmate alone in a cell for a long time, and set up schools in all prisons. She also urged them to get rid of the death penalty.

Several of her ideas were soon put into practice. Jails became less savage places. Men began to say that we should try to *change* those we put away, not just *punish* them. Elizabeth Fry had taught her country to see how cruelly it treated the weak. She had made it a little more kind and understanding, a little more like herself.

Rahere

Rahere was a popular figure at the court of Henry I, the learned youngest son of William the Conqueror. He was a merry, witty fellow who amused his royal master by staging plays and musical entertainments. Some say he was a talented musician who took part in these revels.

When Henry's son was drowned the court plunged into mourning. The prince, only son of the royal couple, was the centre of his father's world. Henry loved the boy with all his heart. He was proud to think that the prince would one day wear his crown.

The king's deep grief lasted until his death. Rahere too was profoundly stirred by the tragedy. His mind turned to religion. He brooded on his sins and the frivolous emptiness of his life. A firm determination to mend his ways seized hold of him. He set out for Rome, the centre of Christendom, to refresh his faith.

When he returned he had a remarkable story to tell. While in Rome he had caught malarial fever. The illness grew worse by the day and soon brought him close to death. He promised God that if he survived he would build a hospital for the poor. Within a short time the fever left him and he embarked on the long journey back to England. On the way home St Bartholomew, one of the twelve apostles, appeared to him in a vision. He instructed Rahere to build a church at Smithfield, at that time a village near London.

The entertainer went to see King Henry, who owned the land the saint had described. The king willingly gave him leave to build a church and a hospital. When Rahere first saw the site his heart sank. Low marshy ground, soggy with undrained water, gave little hope of a firm foundation. The only dry hillock on this dismal plot held a gallows where thieves were hanged.

Rahere was not the man to be beaten by obstacles. He collected helpers, money and building materials. The marsh was swiftly drained. Slowly the hospital and a priory rose on the reclaimed land. Fourteen years of Rahere's life were devoted to keeping his promises to God and the saint. When the hospital opened it had space for a hundred patients. They were poor people who could not afford to pay a doctor. The best medical care of the time was devoted to them. They received good food and – perhaps for the first time – slept in a comfortable bed.

For several years Rahere slaved on, steadily improving the care of his patients. When old age drained his strength he retired to the priory, but he retained to the end his eager interest in the hospital. It has grown considerably through the centuries and is now one of the world's leading hospitals. Nearby, in the priory church of St Bartholomew the Great, lie the bones of Rahere.

Father Damien

When Father Damien went to live on the island of Molokai a hundred years ago he knew that he was sentencing himself to death. His self-imposed task was to minister to six hundred lepers. They were the serious cases sent by the government to the island – one of the Hawaiian group – to prevent them from infecting healthy people. There was no cure for leprosy in those days and its victims slowly and painfully rotted to death.

Father Damien, a thirty-three-year-old Belgian priest, active and muscular, was appalled by what he found there. The lepers were housed in a village of grass huts. There was no doctor. Food and other supplies sent by the government fell hopelessly short of their needs. Drunkenness and violence were commonplace. Many a dying leper watched helplessly as thieves stole his last possessions. And all around this death camp hung an almost unbearable smell – the stench of decaying bodies.

Damien set to work as minister, doctor, nurse, policeman and grave digger. He knew little of medicine but gave his patients drugs sent by doctors from Honolulu. He bandaged their festering sores and buried the dead with his own hands. Angrily he smashed the liquor-jugs. Furiously he scolded the government into sending more supplies. He built an orphanage for boys.

His most important work, however, was to give the lepers hope. God loved them, he repeated in his weekly sermons, and would make up for their hideous sufferings in a better life to come. The death which they awaited was a friend, the gateway to everlasting joy. His words bore fruit. His flock took heart. They learned to face their grim fate with dignity. Drunken brawling and robbery decreased. The lepers tidied up their village in an effort to brighten the short remainder of their lives.

For many years Damien escaped the dread disease. Then one night when he was bathing his hot and painful feet he noticed yellow spots on his arms and back. He knew right away that he had leprosy. The next Sunday he began his sermon: 'We lepers . . .' His listeners understood and were overcome with pity. Their pity was wasted on Father Damien who accepted the blow calmly, almost gladly. 'I want to suffer as Jesus suffered,' he declared.

The brave priest carried on working. Gradually the disease drained his strength. By this time, fortunately, the outside world had learned of Father Damien and many young men and women arrived to help. Inspired by his sacrifice they cheerfully took up his burdens when he closed his eyes for the last time.

Blue for a Boy

No doubt you've heard the saying 'blue for a boy and pink for a girl'. Perhaps you have baby brothers and sisters and noticed that the girls receive presents of pink clothes and the boys of blue. Have you ever wondered how the custom began?

Well, it all started so far back in time that no one knows exactly when. In those days everyone believed in spirits, good and bad. The good spirits brought sunshine and rain, robust health and rich harvests. The bad ones caused storms, disease, death and disasters of every kind.

Now doctors knew much less about illness then than they do today. Many people died because nobody could treat them properly. Lots of babies perished in their cradles because they had the added handicap of not being able to tell where they felt pain. When a baby died the parents often believed that an evil spirit had attacked it. Wicked demons, they thought, floated invisibly over every infant's cot, waiting to pounce.

When parents asked their priests how they could scare away the evil spirits they were told that the child should be dressed in blue, for the demons hated and feared that colour. Blue was the colour of the sky where their enemies, the good spirits, lived. So the parents hurried off and dressed their *boy* babies in blue.

Why, you are asking yourself, did they not dress their *girls* in blue? Well, in those times girls were not as welcome as boys.

Men ruled the world. They claimed to be stronger and smarter than women. Evil spirits could not possibly be interested in harming girls because they were not worth the trouble. For this reason little girls were dressed in no particular colour. Later some kind soul must have thought that it was unfair that girls did not have a special colour of their own, such as pink. So girls finally got their own prettier colour.

Nowadays we know that the idea of evil spirits killing babies is a lot of mumbo-jumbo. And sensible folk know that we should not judge others by whether they are men or women, English or Chinese, black or white.

51

Sir Thomas More

The executioner, hooded and fearsome, waited for his victim, the summer sun glinting on his axe. An excited buzz from the crowd around the scaffold had told him that the sheriff's party was near. Then he saw them, two grim-faced lines of armed men escorting the condemned man. Grey-bearded and weak from illness and imprisonment, he hobbled towards his death. When he reached the stair leading up to the scaffold he stretched out a hand to one of the sheriff's officers. 'Help me up,' he said. 'When I come down again let me shift for myself as well as I can.'

It was the last joke of Sir Thomas More. Minutes later the news of his death was speeding across England and to countries far away. Shocked foreigners asked each other, 'How could the English bring themselves to kill their greatest man?' The answer was: the English did not kill him, their king did.

Thomas More was a Londoner, the lawyer son of a lawyer father. A learned scholar and writer, he was world famous as the author of *Utopia*, an imaginary account of an ideal state. The public knew him as a wise conductor of high affairs of state, his friends as a merry home-lover, deeply devoted to his family and religion.

Henry VIII, impressed by More's great ability, made him Lord Chancellor, a post which carried power second only to his own. More performed his duties scrupul-

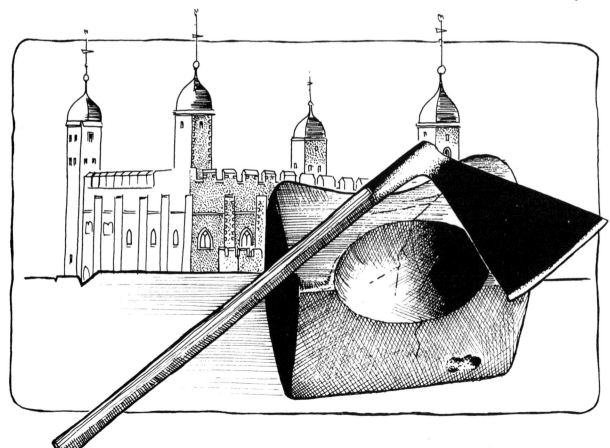

ously. He refused to use his high position to make his fortune, as was common in those days. His fairness was recognized by all.

Craving a son to inherit his throne, Henry asked the pope to dissolve his marriage to his ageing wife Catherine. The pope refused. Furious, Henry made clear his intention of breaking off relations with the Church of Rome. At this Sir Thomas More, who had long spoken and written of the crucial importance of an undivided Church, gave up his office and retired into private life. He was now poor. A parting gift of five thousand pounds was offered to him but he refused it.

Henry divorced Catherine, married Anne Boleyn and declared himself Supreme Head of the Church of England, a body totally separated from the Catholic Church. He ordered his subjects to swear an oath upholding his remarriage and the succession of its children to the throne, and denying the pope's leadership of the Church.

More refused to take the oath. He was thrown in prison and all his lands seized. His wife and children, reduced to poverty, beseeched him to change his mind. Gently he refused. Friends pleaded with him to save himself. An oath, they said, was mere *words*, and an oath sworn under threat of death was not binding. More remained adamant, though frightened for his life.

At his trial he defended himself with all his lawyer's skill but to no purpose. The sentence was death. He died with a joke on his lips, merry to the end. He had given up everything – power, wealth, life itself – for what he believed.

Saviour

The freezing wind screamed through the mountain pass, hurling myriads of hailstones at the travellers. The two men, pulling their hoods down over their faces with blue fingers, staggered along the narrow path, buffeted by the white fury. To stop meant death. A few minutes' rest from the blizzard would leave them frozen forever in the everlasting snows of Tibet. Crouching to lessen the force of the wind, they inched their way along the rough path on sandalled feet. Under their woollen cloaks their bodies shivered in the fearful cold.

The man in front was Sundar Singh. He was a wandering preacher who carried the name of Jesus to the people of India and Tibet. While travelling through the mountains he had caught up with a stranger and they had agreed to journey together. The snowstorm, catching them high up on a steep valley, threatened to bring their trek to a speedy end.

A faint cry reached their ears above the howling of the wind. They looked down and saw a man lying in the snow some way below. He was feebly waving one arm but was plainly badly hurt. 'Quick!' said Sundar, 'we must go down and fetch him. He'll never last five minutes in this.'

'Don't be mad,' his companion shouted. 'We can't carry an injured man.'

'But he'll die if we don't, protested Sundar.

'*We'll* die if we do. Look, if we press on

we might just get through, but if we take him we have no chance. I'm off.' So saying, the stranger tramped off into the storm.

Sundar stepped over the edge of the path on to the ice-covered stones below. Slowly and painfully he lowered himself on to the dangerous stretch. His numb fingers fumbled for secure hand-holds. His sandals probed the glassy surface for safe cracks. The angle of descent grew steeper. Sundar was forced to lie on his side, slithering downward in perilous slow motion. One slip, he knew, could cost him his life.

At last he reached the man. He was unable to move and barely alive. Sundar slung him over his shoulder and started on the climb back to the path. Inch by tortured inch he clawed his way up the slope. The wind, as if angry at being denied its prey, tore at him in mighty gusts. With panting lungs and limbs drained of strength Sundar pushed blindly on. Finally he dragged himself and his burden on to the path and fell exhausted to the ground.

As soon as he felt strong enough Sundar picked up the stranger again. He set off down the narrow way, his legs faltering under their double load. Before long he was staggering from side to side as a deadly tiredness crept through his body. He rounded a corner. Lying against a rock was the travelling-companion who had deserted him. He was dead.

Sundar stumbled on, forcing himself to believe that somehow they might be saved. After a while the wind died down and the going became easier. The path descended to a muddy track that bore the marks of cartwheels. Then came the blessed moment when he saw the lights of a village. The nightmare was over.

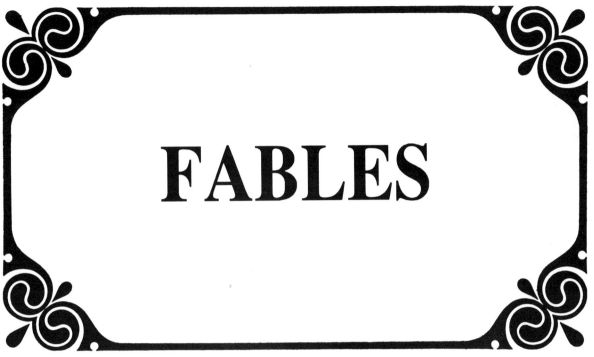

FABLES

Flattery Rewarded

Mother Fox always told her cubs a bedtime story before they went to sleep. One night she told them Aesop's fable about the fox and the crow. In that story a fox spied a crow sitting on the branch of a tree. A tasty piece of cheese was firmly clasped in the bird's bill. The fox decided to have it. He asked the crow to sing to him, for everyone knew what a sweet voice he had. The bird opened his bill and the cheese fell out, to be snapped up by the tricky fellow.

The oldest cub thought that it was the

best story he had ever heard. He kept running over it in his mind during the days that followed. One afternoon he went for a walk in the forest. He happened to glance up at an oak tree. His eyes grew wide with surprise. A crow sat on a low branch holding a long slice of cheese in his beak. The young fox could hardly believe his luck. 'Hello, Brother Crow,' he said cheerfully, 'how are you this fine day?'

The crow nodded a greeting but kept his bill tightly clamped on the cheese. 'I'm told that you're the sweetest singer of all the birds,' the cub continued. 'They say that compared with you the nightingale sounds like a frog. Do let me hear your wonderful voice. A few notes will do.'

The crow stared down, silent. His eyes glittered merrily. If you think I'll fall for that old trick, he seemed to be saying, you never made a bigger mistake in your young life. I wasn't born yesterday. I didn't come up the river in a bubble.

The fox thought quickly. Then he smiled. 'Ah, I can see that you know what I'm up to. I should have known better than to try to fool you with flattery. Everyone says that you're far too sensible to be taken in by false compliments. But tell me, how did you become so strong-minded.'

'It's just a gift I was born with,' said the crow. 'I try to be as modest as I can but —' He stopped, for the moment he opened his bill the cheese fell into the waiting jaws below. After scoffing the dainty snack the fox told him: 'Everyone can be won over by sweet words. You were flattered when I told you that you couldn't be flattered.'

The Magic Fruit

Said the monkey to the pig: 'I need your advice. There's a rumour going around that you're the cleverest of all the animals.'

'I know,' said the pig, 'I started that rumour myself.' He smiled. 'What do you need advice about?'

'Well, I'm just plain unhappy,' replied the monkey. 'I have lots of kind friends, my health is good, I live in one of the better parts of the jungle – no riff-raff, you know – and yet I'm as miserable as sin. Tell me how to become happy.'

The pig thought for a little while. 'You must go and find a zonga tree,' he declared. 'Eat one of its purple fruits and you will be happy forever.'

'A zonga tree!' exclaimed the monkey. 'I've never heard of it, and I've knocked around quite a few trees in my time.'

'I'm not surprised,' said the pig. 'There are only ten in the whole wide world. Off you go now. Find a zonga tree, eat its magic fruit and you'll never know a day's misery again.'

The monkey went off and was absent for a whole year. Every now and then the pig heard news of his journeys. At one time he was reported to be in India. Then came a story that he had settled down in Burma. A swallow swore that he had seen him in London Zoo, or someone very like him.

One summer day the monkey presented himself to the pig. 'How are you, old friend?' he asked warmly.

'Never better, but how are *you*?'

'I've had a marvellous time. I've travelled thousands of miles. It's been jolly hard work but I've seen such fantastic sights, made so many new friends and realized what an exciting world we live in that I've enjoyed every minute of it.'

'But you didn't find the zonga tree?' asked the pig.

The monkey shook his head in mild regret. 'No.'

'That's because there is no such thing,' said the pig. 'My dear fellow, let me explain. Happiness – if there is such a thing – consists in working hard at something you do well. I knew that all you needed was a difficult task among the trees you climb so skilfully. So I made up all that nonsense about the zonga fruit just to keep you busy, and happy. It seems to have worked.'

The monkey confessed: 'It worked all right.'

The Donkey who was Decorated

(Adapted from *Ivan Krilov*)

A farmer said to his donkey, 'You are the best of beasts, a pearl of great price. Of all the donkeys I have owned you are the most hardworking and kind. I shall hang this little bell around your neck so that I shall never lose you.'

The donkey blushed with joy, his grey coat turning a faintly pink shade. Like everyone else he enjoyed being praised. He held out his neck and the farmer placed a blue ribbon over his head. The brass bell tinkled merrily. The donkey was puffed up with pride.

For some days he trotted here and there, making sure that everyone saw and heard the bell. He kept telling himself what a fine fellow he was. Then he found the snags in being a hero. You see, he was not such a good chap as his master thought. He had a sly habit of sneaking into a field when no one was looking to eat some carrots. Now and again he would slip into an orchard and scoff a few apples. He moved with so little noise that he was never found out.

The bell changed all that. The first time he tried to steal an apple the owner, warned by the jolly tinkle, rushed out and beat him black and blue. A few days later a farmer trapped him in his carrot-field and gave him a good – or rather, a bad – whacking. He kept on trying but the bell always gave him away. Its brassy jingle was a sound no farmer could mistake. He might just as well have opened his jaws and brayed with all his power.

By the end of the summer he was stiff and sore from the tips of his ears to the tip of his tail. He made up his mind to stop stealing. Sternly he told himself: 'Aesop was right: pride *does* go before a fall. And another thing, high honours can sometimes bring us to grief.'

Foxed

One day the fox arrived home to find that the autumn winds had blown an old tree right across the entrance to his den. 'Oh dear,' he said, 'if I don't find some way of moving this tree I'll lose my home.' He sat down and gave the matter some thought. Before long he had formed a clever plan.

He hurried over to the bear's cave. The big fellow was about to enter when the fox stopped him. 'Hello, Brother Bear,' he said, smiling with all his charm. 'I'll bet you've never seen a horse without any legs.'

'A horse without legs! Impossible!' growled the bear. 'I could understand a horse losing one leg, or even two legs, but four . . . !' and he turned towards his cave.

'I'll bet you that I can show you one,' said the fox.

The bear stopped. He gave the fox a look that showed his wary mistrust. This is a sly bloke, he told himself, and I have a feeling he's trying to pull a fast one. 'You're on,' he said. 'What do I get if I win?'

'A jar of honey. It's sitting on a shelf in a ruined hut in the woods.'

The bear's eyes lit up with greed. Then he scowled. 'And if I lose?'

'You shift a fallen tree from my den.'

'I agree to the bet,' said the bear. 'If I lose I'll shift the tree, but only after I've had a sleep, for I feel pretty tired and will need all my strength.'

'That suits me fine,' replied the fox.

The crafty fellow led the bear down to the sea. They stood on a flat rock that jutted out over the blue water. 'There you are – a legless horse,' said the fox, pointing into the sea.

The bear stared. A little sea-horse drifted in the clear water, its tail curled around an underwater plant, its back-fin spinning like a tiny windmill. 'But that's not a real horse,' snarled the angry bear.

'Of course it's real,' answered the fox, 'and it has no legs. So I win my bet. I'll call for you tomorrow morning when you've had a good rest. I'll take you to my den and you can move the tree.'

Quivering with rage the bear rushed off without a word. Early next morning the fox went to the cave. There was no sign of the bear so he sat down to wait. A robin flew up and said, 'Brother Bear told me to give you a message. He says he'll shift your tree when he wakes up next spring.'

'But, but . . .' stuttered the fox.

'He told you he would fix the tree after a sleep,' continued the robin, 'but he didn't mention that he intended to sleep the whole winter through, as he always does. He doesn't believe that you have a jar of honey. He advises you to deal honestly with other folk and they will deal honestly with you.'

'I've been swindled,' moaned the crafty one.

'Let's say you've been *foxed*,' said the robin.

The Swan and the Pike

Have you ever seen, in real life or on a postcard, one of those pretty ponds in the country with a graceful swan rippling through its calm waters? No doubt you thought it was a very peaceful scene. Perhaps you even longed to *be* there. Well, it is not always as peaceful as it seems.

There was once just such a picture-postcard pond on whose surface a stately swan floated. Now he was a very bad-tempered fellow. When he saw a mother duck leading her line of ducklings across the pond nothing gave him greater pleasure than to fly at them with a wild hissing and flapping of wings, causing them to scatter in terror. He even attacked a little girl who had brought breadcrumbs to feed him. He struck her with one of his sweeping wings and she ran off howling. He also scared off other birds who landed on the pond, hoping to make their homes there. He boasted that he was the boss of that stretch of water.

Below the surface of the pond there lived another bully. He was the pike. Now the pike is a cannibal fish; that is, he eats other fish. This one was as long as a rifle and nearly as dangerous. He had a huge mouth fitted with teeth like daggers. Most of the time he lay unmoving at the bottom of the pond. Suddenly his grey-green scales would flash in a speedy attack, and

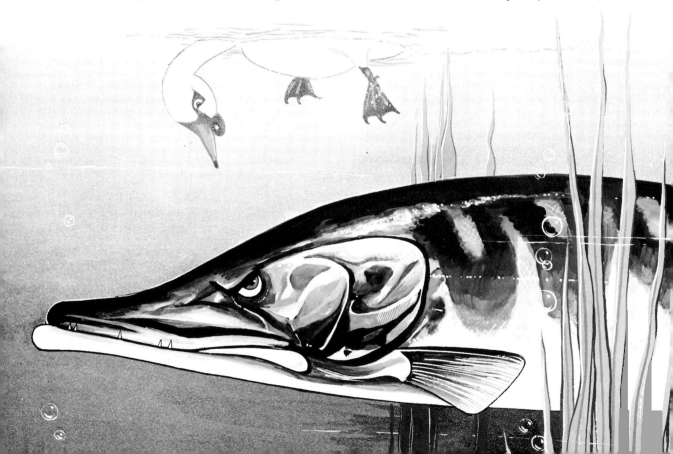

another little fish would vanish inside those roomy jaws. Every creature that lived below the surface of the water feared him, just as those who lived above it dreaded the swan.

Now each of these tyrants came to hear about the other. The swan was furious to be informed that the pike was boss of the pond, for he believed that he was. The pike was just as enraged to hear the same thing said of the swan. Each decided that when he met the other he would show him who really ruled the water.

One day the bullies met. The swan, floating in the middle of the pond, looked down and spied the killer fish directly below. He dived with open beak straight at the eyes. The pike rushed at his enemy with gaping jaws. The swan's head plunged down the pike's throat The fish gave a great gulp to try to swallow the swan. The bird, blinded by the enveloping jaws, pecked savagely about him. The waters of the pond bubbled and heaved wildly as each threw all his strength into the struggle. The swan gasped for air. The pike choked desperately on his bulky enemy. Then all at once the pond was calm again as the two creatures drifted to the bottom – both dead.

'And good riddance!' remarked a duck to a stickleback when they heard the news. 'We're well rid of those yobbos. Perhaps it's really true that all bullies come to a bad end.'

The Spider's Yarn

One night the bat flew into a deep cave to visit the spider, an old friend. 'I see you've finished spinning your web,' he remarked. 'The last time I was here you were having a lot of trouble building it.'

The spider glanced proudly at his finely constructed home. 'I thought I'd never finish it. The trouble was that heavy rains had seeped in and made the cave walls wet. No sooner had I started than a spurt of water washed my yarn away. After this had happened twice I really felt like packing in. Then I remembered what the seagul had told me the day before.

'It seems that the Scottish men and the English men are fighting again. The English have taken over the Scottish land and the Scottish are trying to clear them out. The Scottish king is called Robert Bruce. He has fought six battles against the English and lost the lot. The story goes that he may even risk a seventh.

'Well, when I remembered how hard that man had tried I made up my mind that I would finish my web, no matter how long it took. Men, as you know, are the laziest creatures on earth. I was determined not to be outdone by one of them. So I got stuck in and completed the job at the seventh attempt.'

'What a superb story!' said the bat. 'You certainly spin a wonderful yarn. And what a lesson to us all to keep on trying. It's the kind of tale that may be told a thousand years from now.'

The spider looked gloomy. 'They'll probably tell it all wrong,' he said. 'The older a story becomes the more untrue it is. Besides, I must confess that there was another reason for my slowness in building my web. A tramp was sheltering in the cave at the time and he kept staring at me. I was so nervous that I couldn't work properly. Men sometimes kill other creatures just for fun, and not for food like the rest of us. But he just lay there watching me and when I had finished he got up and strode out. I wonder what became of him.'

Billy Duck's Bed

The fox found it easy to carry off old Farmer Smith's ducks. They slept in the straw in the corner of an old stable. There were holes in the roof and a big gap under the door. Every few weeks the fox slipped into the stable and made off with a plump bird. Farmer Smith was too old or too lazy to repair the holes, so the ducks lived in fear.

One day a clever young duck named Billy said to his friend Steve, 'We must find somewhere safer to sleep. While we're in that tumbledown stable we're sitting ducks, if you'll pardon the expression. Now, I have an idea. Why not use the dog's basket? It's been lying idle in the yard since Rover died.'

'You must be mad,' said Steve. 'The fox would simply stroll into the yard and snatch you from the basket.'

'Listen,' said Billy, 'here's what we'll do. You know the old swing that hangs from the oak tree – the one the children used to swing on before they grew up and left? Well, we'll fly up on to the seat and nibble through the ropes so that the seat drops off. Then we'll push the dog's basket under the ropes. With a bit of effort we can tie it to the ropes in place of the seat. Next we'll flap our way up the tree and out along the branch. We'll pull the ropes up and tie them firmly. That will give us a

plan and asked for his help. 'Not me,' said Donald, 'I um, ah, suffer from a fear of heights. I couldn't sleep five feet from the ground without feeling dizzy. Try some of the others.'

Billy tried every duck but each one had a different excuse for not helping. He made up his mind to do the job alone. He started at noon. All through the afternoon and evening he sweated, and as night fell he finished his task. Proudly he flew up into the dog's basket, watched by a circle of smiling friends. Then he closed his eyes and was soon asleep.

He was wakened by the sound of someone quacking his name. He looked down and saw that it was Steve. 'The fox pounced last night,' gasped Steve, 'and snatched two ducklings. Please let me sleep in your basket from now on.'

'But what about your bad back? No, I couldn't possibly let you sleep up here. I'd never forgive myself if you made your poor back even worse.'

At that moment Donald arrived. 'I've changed my mind,' he announced. 'I'd like to sleep up there, if you don't mind.'

'What, and make yourself ill with your fear of heights,' said Billy. 'No, it's kind of you to offer to keep me company but I couldn't put your health at risk.'

Steve and Donald begged to be allowed to use the basket. Donald explained that his illness was getting better all the time and Steve claimed that his bad back had improved overnight. Finally Billy, a soft-hearted fellow who had only been teasing his friends, agreed to share his sleeping quarters. But he could not resist telling them: 'If you want something, work for it.'

sleeping basket low enough for us to fly into every night, but too high for the fox to reach. It will be hard work but you and I can do it. Shall we start now?'

Steve replied, 'No, I don't think I will. I er, um, have a bad back that prevents me from flying. Ask someone else.'

So Billy approached Donald, the strongest duck on the farm, explained his

The Solitary Sycamore

Near the edge of the forest lived a small cluster of sycamore trees. When autumn came, chilling the air and covering the earth with fallen leaves, the trees put out little bunches of winged seeds. One seed, who was for some reason prouder than the others, declared: 'When my time comes to fly away I intend to get as far from this dump as I can. I'm not just going to be one tree in a thousand. None of these old sycamores around us is going to tell *me* how to behave. No sir, you won't catch me living a dreary life in this neck of the woods.'

He waited patiently for a high wind. It was a long time coming. Although the night frosts had begun to ice over the forest pools the weather stayed calm. All his brother seeds had dropped off, settling on the ground close by. Then one day a mighty wind roared through the forest, bending the bare trees and scattering withered leaves. The proud seed hurled himself into the air. Up and up he swirled like a tiny helicopter, borne by the wild blast. He rushed away from the forest, down the hill, and came to earth in a meadow. Imagine his joy when he found that the nearest tree was a hundred metres away.

Quickly he put down roots in the rich grassland. They spread wide and deep, for they did not have to fight for space with the roots of other trees. The sycamore became first a sturdy sapling and then a strong young tree. 'I stand alone,' he told himself with some pride, 'just as I set out to do.'

Then he found that living on his own had its drawbacks. Chief of these was loneliness. He had no one to talk to. He began to long for the cosiness of the forest, where the trees whisper to each other all day long. The icy winds of winter seemed to bear down on him alone. His brothers and sisters, he knew, enjoyed some shelter from bitter weather by living in a crowd.

Worse was to come. As soon as he was tall enough the village children gladly swarmed all over him. Their shoes scratched painfully along his bark. Merrily they hacked off his branches for firewood. 'What a blunder I made!' said the miserable sycamore. 'There's no happiness in living alone, far from my own kind, and there's nothing I can do about it.'

The Shy Tern

Once upon a time there was a handsome young tern who lived with thousands of other seabirds on a rocky island not far from the shore. His wings were long and narrow, his bill entirely black and his tail forked. The white feathers of his slender chest showed just a hint of pink. He was fully grown and an expert catcher of fish

One day Tommy, the oldest tern on the island, flew up to him. 'Look here, young fellow,' he said, 'don't you think it's about time you settled down and took a wife. There are hundreds of pretty young females flying about. Surely there must be at least one who has caught your eye.'

The young tern blushed and mumbled: 'Well, I . . . yes, there is a beautiful young bird I would dearly love to spend the rest of my life with. But I am painfully shy. I cannot even bring myself to speak to her, let alone ask her to set up home with me.'

'Now listen to me,' said the old chap in his sternest tone. 'Half the trouble in this world is caused by folk who demand more than they deserve. The other half is caused by creatures who are too timid to ask for what they are entitled to. They become angry with themselves and take it out on others. Take my word for it, they cause just as much misery as the grabbers. You must not let that happen to you. Go straight away to that young one and ask her to be your bride.'

These strong words put fresh heart into the handsome bird. He flew at once to the high rock where his sweetheart was preening herself and asked her to be his mate. To his delighted amazement she consented on the spot. Together they flew off to build their home, watched by Tommy and his wife. The wife remarked: 'They'll make a fine young couple.'

'One good tern deserves another,' said Tommy.

A Cheetah Protests

The wise old lion said to his young ones, 'Cubs, you would be amazed at what silly things we animals will believe in order not to face the truth about ourselves. Let me tell you about the cheetah and the jungle Olympics.

'He entered for the sprint event which he had won in record time at the last games. Naturally he won again, for you know how speedy he is. But he was very disappointed when his time was announced – seventeen beats. I should explain that we measure time by the number of the hummingbird's heartbeats. Anyway, he approached me – I was chairman of the games – and protested about the time. "It's ridiculous!" he shouted. "I did it in fifteen beats last time and I'm faster now than I was then."

'I told him as gently as I could: "You're a splendid sprinter but you're four years older than you were then. We all slow up as we get on in years, even world-beaters like you."

'He scoffed at that. "There's been a mistake," he said. "The cockerel announced the wrong time. I demand to see the figures set down by the clerk of the games." Well, I took him along to the secretary-bird and she produced the leaf on which she had pecked the result of the sprint. There it was in black and green – seventeen beats.

'Off he stormed in a huff. Next day he was back, smiling. "I see now why I seem to be slower. You see, the hummingbird's heartbeat quickens as it grows older. So fifteen beats four years ago is really the

same as seventeen today." Now, I know nothing about the workings of our bodies so I took him along to the dragon, who is an expert. The dragon – he likes to be known as Dr Agon – declared: "That's nonsense! The bird's heart beats at the same rate throughout its life." Well, you should have seen the cheetah dash off through the long grass, choked with rage.

'A few days later he was back with another idea. He claimed that someone must have moved the big rock that marked the starting point. That meant that he had run forty or fifty paces farther than last time. Naturally it took him longer. We went to examine the rock. It was covered with moss, and so deeply embedded in the ground that it had not moved for centuries. The cheetah slunk off so sadly that I really thought I had heard the end of the matter.

'He came to see me the very next night, excited and happy. "I was right after all," he said. "I overheard two men talking yesterday. One was explaining to the other that the whole of creation is expanding. All the stars are rushing away from each other at a fearful speed. So it follows that our Earth is swelling. This means that the distance between any two points is growing all the time. So I really did run much farther and that explains why I took longer."'

The oldest cub, who had been listening to this story with close attention, asked, 'And didn't you tell him he was talking crazy rubbish?'

'No,' said his father. 'I had as much chance of making him face the truth as the snail had of winning the high jump.'

What Everyone Gives

A rabbit on his way home to his burrow came across a field-mouse sitting beside a well. It was an old-fashioned well – just a hole in the ground – whose sides sloped steeply down to a circle of water. 'I'm dying for a drink,' said the field-mouse plaintively, 'but I'm afraid to slip on the wet ground and finish up in the water.'

'I'll tell you what to do,' said the rabbit. 'Nip over to the marshy ground near the lake and pull out a long reed. Bring it back here and nibble off both ends. You'll find that the stem is hollow. Put one end in the water and you can suck it up from a safe distance.'

The field-mouse looked doubtful. 'That's an awful lot of trouble. No, I think I'll be safe enough if I creep carefully down to the water's edge.'

'Please yourself,' said the rabbit, and he lolloped off. He had not gone ten metres when – splash – the field-mouse tumbled into the water. Smiling and shaking his head, the rabbit went on his way. Soon he met a dog who was staring mournfully at a beehive. 'What's the matter?' inquired the rabbit.

'I buried some juicy bones in this field,' said the dog. 'Then the farmer placed a beehive right over the spot where they lie.

Now I'm afraid to dig under the beehive in case I disturb the bees and they attack me.'

The rabbit thought for a moment. 'You must wait until night falls. When it's dark you can dig the bones up safely. Bees don't come out at night.'

'I can't wait that long,' replied the dog. 'No, I'll just start digging boldly. I'll show the bees that I'm their master, as the farmer does. Besides, I have a thick coat to protect me.'

'Please yourself,' said the rabbit, and off he went. Almost at once the air was filled with howls of pain. The rabbit turned to see the dog running madly across the field pursued by an angry cloud of bees. He grinned all the way home to his burrow on a steep bank near the river.

As soon as he reached the bank his smile vanished. His burrow had been covered by a fall of loose earth. The hole was nowhere to be seen. He began to dig furiously towards the entrance, his paws throwing up sprays of damp earth.

'I shouldn't do that if I were you,' said a voice above him.

The rabbit looked up. A crow was addressing him from a nearby tree. 'That bank has been soaked by heavy rain,' continued the bird, 'and it's in a very shaky state. If you carry on digging into it you're likely to bring the whole thing down about your floppy ears.'

'Nonsense,' snorted the rabbit. 'How could a little fellow like me bring down a great chunk of earth like that? I'll dig my way in, if it's all the same to you.'

'Please yourself,' said the crow.

The rabbit started again. So swiftly did his paws fly that within a very short time he had found the entrance to his home. Then crash! The bank fell on him. At first he lay stunned and breathless. Then, as his strength returned, he began to dig his way blindly out towards the light. The struggle to escape was long and tiring. At last, however, he clawed his way to safety and lay gasping for breath.

The crow spoke. 'Here's a riddle: what is it that everyone gives and no one takes?'

'Advice,' groaned the rabbit.

The Heron

The heron is a large wading-bird. He feeds on fish which he catches with his long bill. One day a heron was standing on the bank of a river. Looking into its depths he saw many fat fish gliding here and there. He was so close that he could easily have scooped one out. He was sharply tempted to do so but thought, 'No, I'll wait till my usual lunchtime. I'll be really hungry then.' Off he flew to visit his friend who lived near the windmill.

When lunchtime came he arrived back on the river bank. 'Now for a delicious meal of fleshy carp,' he said. But when he looked into the water all the carp had gone. The only fish in sight were tench, which are much smaller than carp. 'I'm

not going to eat tench,' said the heron to himself. 'I'll wait for a while and see if the big ones come back.'

So he flew twice around the mountain. By this time he was very hungry indeed and could hardly wait to get his bill into a well-fed fish. But he thought, 'If the carp haven't come back I suppose I'll just have to be satisfied with tench. Mind you, tiddlers like those don't deserve to be eaten by a fine bird like me but sometimes we all have to put up with second best.'

He got a sickening surprise when he went back to the river and found that all the tench had left. The only fish he could see were little gudgeons, so small that they were not worth catching. Sadly he wandered off. He walked up and down the bank of the river searching eagerly for a fish of fair size to fill his stomach and stop his hunger pains. Soon darkness fell and he could not even see whether any were still swimming about. He gave up the hunt and turned to go.

At that moment he spied a tiny slug crawling on a stone. You could say that a slug is a snail without a shell. It has a very nasty taste. Without wasting a second the heron snatched it up and swallowed it. He had never eaten one before, for he believed that humble creatures like slugs were no meal for the likes of him. Then he flew off to his nest saying, 'From now on I'll take my opportunities when they come. Good chances don't come very often and when they do we should grab them.'

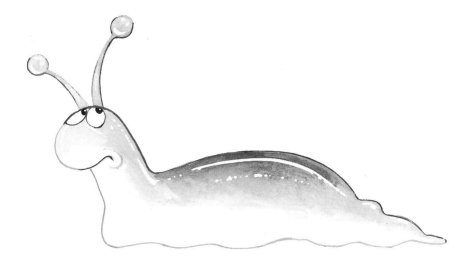

Sidney and Sammy Squirrel

Mrs Squirrel said to her twin sons Sidney and Sammy, 'Now children, you're old enough to leave home and set up house for yourselves. You know how to make a home, as you've seen me do it. I just want to remind you of two things before you go. First, don't live near the humans. They have long sticks that can make a terrible bang and kill you stone dead. Second, you must always remember to lay in a good supply of nuts for the winter. Otherwise you could starve to death. Do you hear me, Sidney?'

'Yes, mother,' said Sidney, who always listened to his mother's advice.

'Are you listening, Sammy?'

'Er, yer,' said Sammy, but in fact Sammy had been thinking of how marvellous life would be in his own home, far from his mother's scolding tongue.

'Goodbye, boys,' said Mrs Squirrel, wiping a tear from the corner of her eye.

Sidney searched the wood for the best home he could find. He wanted a comfortable hole high and safe in a tall tree. It must be near a good number of nut trees. It must *not* be too close to the housing estate where the humans lived. If possible it should be close to running water. At last he found the perfect home in a high tree.

He made it cosy by lining the hole with grasses and twigs. Then, remembering his mother's parting advice, he began to lay in a stock of nuts for the winter.

In the meantime his brother Sammy had been acting very differently. He set up house in the first hole he found, which happened to be quite near the houses. His days were spent in swinging through the trees all over the woods. Often he sat for hours watching the humans at their strange pastimes. Now and then he stayed up until after dark, for he had always promised himself that when he was master of his own house he would stay up as late as he liked. Throughout the autumn he munched nuts until he grew fat but he did not bother to lay in a store of them.

Suddenly, when he woke one morning, winter was upon him. The world was white with snow and the nut trees were bare. He huddled, hungry and frozen, in his home for as long as he could but at last he said to himself, 'I must go to Sidney and see if he can give me some food to tide me over the winter.'

Off he set. When he reached Sidney's tree he found his mother there, sobbing bitterly. 'The fox has got him,' she cried. 'The rascal's clever enough to know that sensible squirrels make their homes as far from the houses as they can. So every year he comes to this end of the wood to hunt for young squirrels. You may have his home now if you want it, Sammy.'

Sammy was sorry about his brother but glad to climb into Sidney's comfortable home with its rich store of nuts. As he curled up and prepared to sleep through the winter he could not help thinking that everything had worked out very nicely.

Now this story ends very badly, don't you think? Sidney, the wise fellow who did all the right things, should have lived happily ever after and Sammy – light-hearted, silly Sammy – should have come to a sticky end. But in real life things sometimes turn out that way. Hardworking folk are left with nothing while idlers walk off with the prizes.

STORIES FROM SACRED BOOKS

A Hard Case

(Adapted from *The Midrash*)

'I swear I returned the money to this man,' said Bar Talmion.

'And I tell you he didn't,' asserted the other.

Rabbi Asse rubbed his chin with thumb and forefinger, as he always did when he was puzzled. How could one tell which of these men was lying? He had sat in his judge's chair patiently listening to both sides, and he must deliver his judgement soon. He ran over the facts of the case in his mind.

A man had taken Bar Talmion, a money-dealer, to court. He claimed that he had given the dealer a sum of money to keep safely for him. When he had asked for it back Bar Talmion declared that he had already returned it. Each man claimed flatly that the other was lying.

Rabbi Asse, still undecided, spoke to Bar Talmion: 'You *swear* you gave him the money?'

'I certainly do.'

'Will you swear *on oath* in the synagogue?'

'Yes.'

The judge leaned forward. 'An oath means calling on God to witness that what you say is true. Bearing that in mind, are you still willing to take it?'

'*Willing?*' snorted the money-dealer, 'I *insist* on taking it to clear my good name.'

The rabbi rose and left the court with the two men who were in dispute. He led them to the synagogue, the Jewish place of worship. As they were about to enter, Bar Talmion handed his walking-stick to the plaintiff. 'Hold this for me while I take the oath,' he said. The man took the stick and was surprised at its weight. Surely this is too heavy for a walking-stick, he thought. Then he noticed a thin crack running all the way round near the top. He twisted the handle and it came off, revealing that the stick was hollow. He turned it upside-down. A cascade of gold coins tinkled to the flagstones.

For Bar Talmion the game was up. He intended to swear on oath that he had given back the money. By handing over his stick he would be telling the strict truth. Later he would take back the stick and get away with the swindle. But there is no doubt that the oath he planned to swear would have been a false one. Truth is not just words.

Martha and Mary

One evening Jesus arrived at a village called Bethany, tired and hungry. He made his way to the house of Martha and Mary where he knew he would be made welcome. The two women, delighted to see their old friend and teacher, ushered him into the most comfortable chair next to the fire. Mary sat at his feet and instantly began to ply him with questions about his stories and teachings. Her sister fetched a tall, wide-bellied jar from which she poured cool water into a bowl. At her invitation Jesus gratefully washed away the dust of his day's travel, all the while answering Mary's questions with the confident cleverness that had made him the talk of the land.

When Jesus sat down at the fire again Martha busied herself making the supper. It would have to be a very special meal, she told herself, for Jesus was a very special person. As she bustled around at her task she listened as he explained himself, making the most difficult ideas seem simple by the use of little stories of country life. Mary, she noted with annoyance, had not moved from her place at Jesus' feet to lend a hand with the supper. She sat with her legs tucked under her and the firelight brightened her face as she listened, wide-eyed.

Soon the meal was ready. Well-cooked food on Martha's best dishes covered the table. She would have been pleased at the result of her work but for her anger at her sister's idleness. She could keep silent no longer. 'Lord,' she said, 'don't you think it's a shame that Mary leaves me to do all the work. Tell her to give me a hand with the household chores. She'll listen to you.'

Jesus, surprised, thought for a moment before replying. 'Look, Martha, I know you work hard at running this house. That's important, for *somebody* must do these tiring, boring jobs. But Mary is right. It is more important to listen to me and learn how to live a good life.'

We do not know if Martha made any answer. Perhaps she said, 'In that case *I* shall sit at the fire after supper while *she* does the washing-up.'

Confucius on Leadership

(Adapted from *The Book of Lieh-tzu*)

Confucius was famous throughout China for his wisdom. It came as no surprise to anyone when he was appointed mayor of the city of Chang-tu. He quickly showed his skill as a ruler and his ability to manage the officials under him. It was clear that he was not just a clever talker.

Soon after he took up his post a friend named Hsia called to see him. Hsia was curious about the kind of men who worked for Confucius.

'What sort of a person is Yen Hui?' he asked.

'He is a kinder man than I am,' replied Confucius.

'What do you think of Kung?' queried Hsia.

The mayor thought for a while. 'He's a much better speaker than I.'

'What about Lu?'

'He has more courage than I.'

'And what sort of man is Chang?' asked Hsia.

'As far as dignity is concerned, he's better than I am.'

Hsia smiled in a puzzled kind of way. 'Look here, if these men are so much better than you why are they serving you and not you them?'

Confucius smiled back. 'It's quite simple. Yen Hui is kind, but sometimes kindness is not the answer to a problem. Now and then a true leader must do things which offend people. Kung is a wonderful speaker but doesn't know when to stop. Lu's bravery often spurs him into rash action when caution is needed. It is vital to know when to act swiftly and when to move slowly. Indeed, it is sometimes best to do nothing. Chang is dignified but cannot relax and be friendly, as we all must do at times.

'A wise leader should possess all the virtues shown by these men, but in the right blend. No single quality should overrule the others. The mind of a ruler should, like an excellent meal, contain the best ingredients in the correct amounts.'

Just Desserts

(Adapted from *The Talmud*)

Hadrian, Emperor of Rome, was walking in the country when he saw an old farmer planting a fig tree. The emperor, who often enjoyed the tasty little fruit, was surprised to find a man so far gone in years at work in the fields. 'How old are you?' he asked.

'A hundred,' came the reply.

Hadrian's eyebrows rose in amazement. 'But at your great age – if you don't mind my saying so – you're unlikely to live to gather the fruit.'

'If it's God's wish,' said the old man, 'I'll eat these figs. If it's not, I'll leave them to my son, as my father before me left them to me. I place myself entirely in God's hands.'

The emperor was impressed by the man's simple faith. 'Well, perhaps you'll bring me some and we'll enjoy eating them together – that is, if we're both spared.'

'I don't see why not,' answered the farmer. 'You look pretty healthy to me.'

Laughing heartily, the emperor left, never expecting to see the old man again. But he did. A few years later the ancient farmer entered the palace carrying a basket full of delicious figs. Hadrian made him welcome, ate some of the ripe fruit and declared it excellent. Then he emptied the remaining figs into a bowl and filled the basket with gold coins. The old farmer thanked him sincerely and left for his home in the country.

Now the wife of one of the man's neighbours heard about the emperor's lavish gift. She urged her husband to take a basket of figs to Hadrian so that he too might be rewarded. The greedy fellow needed no persuading. He at once picked his most juicy fruits and set out for the palace.

He was gone for several days. When he returned his wife was astonished at his appearance. His face and robe were stained with fig-juice and his skin bore many small bruises. He slumped into a chair. 'When I got to the palace,' he moaned, 'I asked the guards to empty my basket and fill it with gold. They promptly informed the emperor. He was furious. He ordered me to stand in the courtyard while his servants pelted me with figs.'

The wife, though disappointed, could not help smiling at her husband's miserable face. 'Try to look on the bright side,' she advised. 'You might have taken coconuts.'

Bringing Back the Cat

(Adapted from *The Panchatantra*)

When the world was a good deal younger there lived four priests in an Indian village. They had grown up together and were good friends. Three of them were men who had gained immense learning by wide reading and hard thinking. The other was no scholar but possessed a deep fund of common sense.

As their knowledge increased the three clever priests became more and more dissatisfied with village life. 'Our talents are wasted in this place,' said one. 'Let's go to the king and offer him our skills. He'll be only too glad to use fine brains like ours.' The others were of the same mind so they prepared for the journey to the palace. At the last moment they decided to take their friend with them. Of course he would be of no value to the king, they agreed, but they might as well take him along for old times' sake.

On their way through the forest they came across a heap of large bones. 'These are the remains of a large animal,' stated the first priest.

'They're the bones of a lion,' said the down-to-earth priest, who had often

watched the hunters stalk lions while his friends were at their books.

The first man went on: 'I can arrange these bones so that they form a complete skeleton of the beast.'

'And I have the skill to give that skeleton flesh, blood and skin,' claimed the second.

The third priest was trembling with excitement. 'I could make such a creature come back to life.'

They set to work with expert energy. The fourth priest watched, his forehead wrinkled in a worried frown. When the lion was re-formed and the third priest about to breathe new life into it, he spoke up. 'Look here, friends, you realize what you're doing? Lions are savage animals. If he comes back to life —'

'Be quiet, you fool,' snapped the first man. 'Can't you see we're making history – giving life to the dead!'

'Please listen to me,' begged the fourth priest. 'Believe me, I know a good deal about lions.'

'You don't know nearly as much as we do. We have read all the books. You haven't.'

His friend shrugged his shoulders. 'It's your funeral. Excuse me while I shin up the nearest tree.' He suited the action to the word and watched the rest of the operation seated on a high branch.

Suddenly the lion opened his eyes, roared, fell on the priests and killed all three. The fourth man sadly remarked: 'I've said it before and I'll say it again: all the learning in the world is useless without plain, ordinary common sense.'

The Bramble Bush

(Adapted from *The Masnavi*)

Omar was a lazy, good-natured man with a taste for practical jokes. One night, when the villagers were asleep, he slipped out and dug a hole in the street. He planted a little bramble bush and carefully patted the loose earth firmly into place around its roots. Then, laughing silently at his naughtiness, he stole back to bed.

At first no one in the Arab village noticed the bush. Barefoot children played around it and camels stepped on it, flattening its thin stems. But before long its roots grew strong. The bush swelled into a bulky plant with sweeping stems and long, sharp thorns. Then everyone noticed it. Children howled with pain when it scratched their feet. Camels walked into it by accident and reared up, often throwing their riders to the dust. Old men declared that it was a disgrace to the village and should be removed at once. All of a sudden everyone wanted to know who had planted the bush.

There could be only one answer – Omar the joker. The mayor stormed up to him and asked him point-blank if he had done it. Shamefacedly Omar admitted that he had. 'Well, dig it up at once,' roared the mayor.

'I'll do it as soon as I've fixed my spade,' Omar promised.

A week passed. The bramble still stood, its thorns causing as much pain and annoyance as ever. The mayor was enraged. 'When are you going to get rid of that confounded nuisance?' he hissed.

'Oh, er, ah,' stuttered Omar, 'I'll do it on Monday, or perhaps Tuesday.'

On Wednesday the plant was still there. 'My dear Omar,' said the mayor wearily, 'you can't put off uprooting that bush any longer. You're just bone-lazy.'

'It's my bad back,' protested Omar. 'As soon as it's better I'll get rid of that bramble. I'll dig it up in a few days, almost certainly.'

But he did not. The mayor scolded him. Omar made one excuse, then another promise. He did not keep it. Every day that passed saw the bramble grow larger and more prickly. The mayor complained again and again, and Omar swore each time that he would do the job soon. The bush remained untouched.

One day the mayor said, 'My dear man, can't you see the harm you're doing – not just to your friends and neighbours but to yourself? As the days slip by that bush grows stronger and you grow weaker. The longer you put off digging it up the harder the job will be. A man of your age must know that putting off unpleasant tasks is a foolish habit. If you do not fight against it, it will grow inside you like the bramble bush until it is too strong to be rooted out. And as the bramble chokes other plants that grow near it, so your idleness will smother all your good qualities.'

The old story ends there. I wonder if Omar was won over by the clever speech.

Grapes

Four men set out together to travel to a distant city. One was Turkish, another Persian, the third an Arab and the fourth was Greek. None spoke the language of any of the others. However, they were glad of each other's company, for it was dangerous to travel alone in those faraway days. They managed to make their meaning clear to each other by miming and drawing pictures in the sand, but soon they all began to feel the strain of not being able to chat.

Luck was with them. They fell in with a fifth traveller who was journeying to the same city. He was a Sufi, a member of a religion which values the great truths in all faiths. Being an expert at languages he could speak all their tongues. Eagerly they invited him to join their little band. He was glad to do so.

They went on their way. The new man translated all their remarks into the languages of the others, so the days were filled with merry chatter. One day when they were drawing near the city the Sufi left his friends to visit a cousin who lived nearby. He rejoined them in the afternoon in a village fruit and vegetable market. To his surprise he found them purple-faced with anger, shouting at each other. They had used up all their money except one silver coin and were arguing about what they should spend it on.

'*Uzum*,' insisted the Turk.

'No, no, *angur*,' roared the Persian.

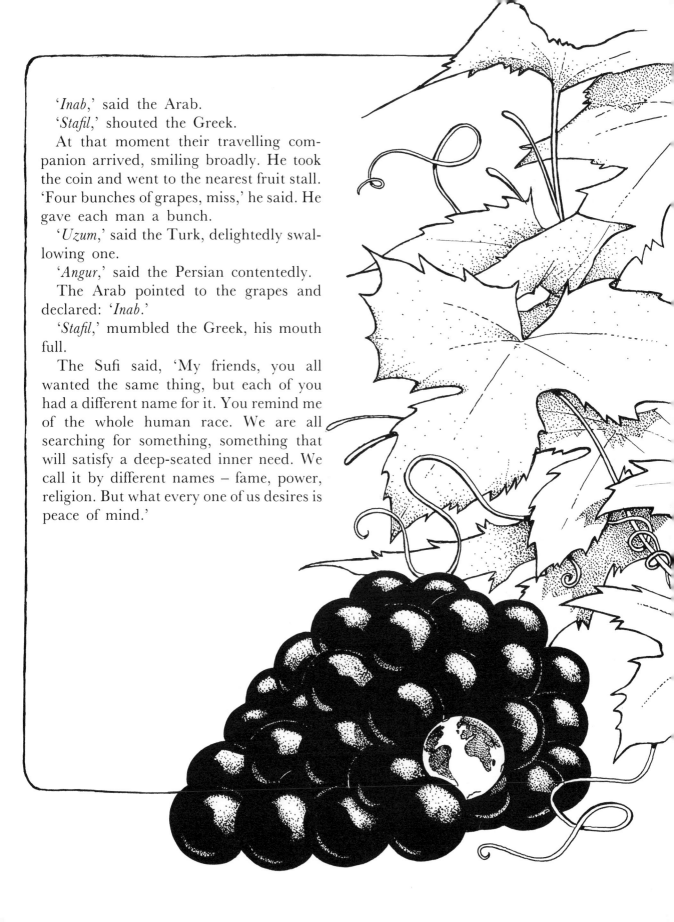

'*Inab*,' said the Arab.

'*Stafil*,' shouted the Greek.

At that moment their travelling companion arrived, smiling broadly. He took the coin and went to the nearest fruit stall. 'Four bunches of grapes, miss,' he said. He gave each man a bunch.

'*Uzum*,' said the Turk, delightedly swallowing one.

'*Angur*,' said the Persian contentedly.

The Arab pointed to the grapes and declared: '*Inab*.'

'*Stafil*,' mumbled the Greek, his mouth full.

The Sufi said, 'My friends, you all wanted the same thing, but each of you had a different name for it. You remind me of the whole human race. We are all searching for something, something that will satisfy a deep-seated inner need. We call it by different names – fame, power, religion. But what every one of us desires is peace of mind.'

The Founding of a Tradition

(Adapted from a story by Sheikh Qualander Shah)

In a land across the sea there is an old village where no one lives. Weeds grow on the roofs of ruined houses and grass carpets the streets. It is a small village – just two parallel streets linked by a narrow lane – like a capital H. If you ask anyone who lives nearby how the place came to be deserted you will hear an odd tale.

A long time ago five hundred people lived in the busy village. One afternoon a Sufi, a wise and holy man, was seen walking along the lane that led from one street to the other. His eyes were full of tears. Down his cheeks ran two tiny rivers that splashed wet spots on to his white robe. On reaching the second street he headed slowly towards the open countryside. The villagers watched him, shocked. No one dared to ask him the reason for his tragic appearance. The mayor guessed: 'Someone has died in the other street.' A woman whispered: 'Could it be the plague?' A young girl began to cry. She knew what the plague was – a deadly disease that could spread quickly and kill all it touched. Soon the street was in an uproar. Everyone was

certain that the plague had struck. At once there was a frantic scramble to leave the village. Donkeys and handcarts were loaded in an instant, and within an hour there was not a soul to be seen in the street.

Meanwhile the other street had also emptied. The people who lived there had heard the shouts of 'Plague' and run for the hills without a second thought. When night fell there was not a man, woman or child in the place.

They never went back. Their village rotted. Desert foxes crept in and set up home in empty houses. Birds nested without fear in the straw roofs. Two new villages grew up not far away.

One day the mayor, while strolling in the street, met the Sufi whose tears had caused his people to quit their homes. 'Why *were* you crying that day?' he asked.

'I wasn't crying,' came the reply. 'I had been peeling onions and they always make my eyes water.'

The mayor's mouth dropped open in astonishment.

'I hope you've learned your lesson,' said the Sufi. 'Tiny rumours grow larger as they pass from mouth to mouth, like a snowball rolling down a hill. You mustn't believe anything unless you have some evidence for doing so.'

Chuang Wags his Tail

(Adapted from *The Chuang-tzu*)

On an afternoon long ago Chuang Tze sat on the river bank, his back supported by a willow tree, his fishing line trailing in the water. He was barefoot and his clothes were shabby and none too clean. From under his straw hat, which was comically tilted over his forehead, he lazily watched two men cross the wooden bridge upstream. Their rich clothes and air of importance told him they were high officials. His eyes followed them as they made their way towards him, daintily stepping around the puddles on the muddy bank, their hands tucked into their wide sleeves.

When they reached him the older one spoke: 'Greetings from our master, the great Prince Wei, to the admirable Chuang Tze. He is filled with wonder at your wisdom. You have spread the golden words of our Tao religion to the four corners of China. Our master has heard that you despise riches and even the simplest bodily comforts. So great is his esteem for you that he invites you to become the prime minister of his country.'

Chuang Tze did not even look up. 'I have been told,' he began, 'that the prince has countless treasures, but none he values more highly than a sacred tortoise which died three thousand years ago. They say he keeps it locked in an ornamental box on the altar of his forefathers. There he prays every day, like every good Chinaman, to the spirits of the dead. Now do you think that tortoise would prefer to be dead and have his corpse prayed over by a prince, or alive and wagging his tail in the mud?'

'There can be only one answer,' said the younger official. 'It would rather be alive.'

'Go away then,' said Chuang. 'I too prefer to wag my tail in the mud.'

The two men left, in no doubt of the wise man's meaning. Chuang regarded the post of prime minister as a kind of ornamental box that drew respect but enclosed a dead spirit. Far more vital to him was to say what he liked and act as he pleased.

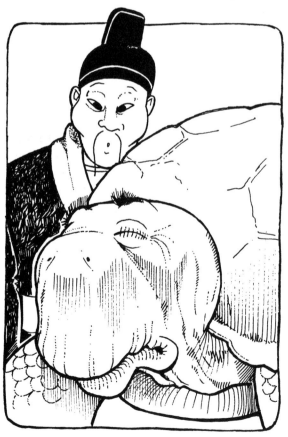

Are Old Men Wise?

(Adapted from *The Talmud*)

Back in the old days a rich man sent his only son to Jerusalem to study under a wise teacher. Not long after the young man left home his father fell ill. His condition quickly grew worse and it became clear that he had not long to live. With a faltering hand he wrote a new will, leaving everything he owned to one of his slaves on condition that he allowed the son to choose one item for himself. A few days later he died.

The very next day the delighted slave hurried up to Jerusalem and showed the will to the son. The young man was thunderstruck. He took the will to his teacher and read it to him. 'Have you ever heard anything like it?' he exclaimed bitterly. 'I loved my father deeply and I believed he loved me too. I never did anything to offend him and yet he leaves me penniless.'

The old teacher read the document slowly. Then he looked up, a strange little smile playing around his mouth. 'Your father was a wise and loving parent,' he said, 'and this will proves how much he cared for you. I only hope you have half his common sense when you grow up.'

'You're joking!' gasped the youngster. 'He gives all his property to a *slave*, leaving his only son flat broke, and you call him *wise*. I'm sick of hearing how wise old people are. I think it's all a yarn put about by old folk themselves to impress the rest of us.'

'Listen to me,' said the teacher, 'and I'll tell you exactly what happened. Your father, knowing his death was near, decided to make sure that you would inherit all his possessions. But he saw the folly of naming you as his heir. As soon as

he died his slaves would steal everything they could, for your absence would make it easy for them. Indeed, they would take their time about telling you of his death to give themselves more time for plundering. So he left his property to one slave, knowing that he would protect it and let you know the contents of the will right away.'

The young man looked bewildered. 'But how does that benefit me?'

'Look, your father left you the right to choose one article from all he owned. You must choose the slave himself, for he was part of the old man's property.'

'Yes, but I don't see —'

'The law is quite clear,' explained the old teacher patiently. 'Everything a slave owns belongs to his master. If you take him as your share you will become his master, and therefore the owner of all his possessions. In that way you will inherit your father's wealth as he intended you to.'

A look of understanding slowly flooded the youngster's face. 'I take back all I said about old people pretending to be wise.'

His teacher smiled. 'It's not that we're any cleverer than the young. It's just that we've lived longer, seen more, thought more.'

The young man did as he had been advised and recovered his father's riches. He then gave the slave his freedom to console him for his loss.

Goods Beyond Price

(Adapted from *The Midrash*)

The cargo boat set sail for a distant port, its hold crammed with goods of every sort. The merchants who owned the goods were on board, for they wished to sell their wares in person. On the first night at sea they fell into conversation with a stranger who did not seem to be one of their number. His cheap clothes led them to think that he was not nearly as well-off as themselves. One trader asked him what kind of goods he dealt in. He replied, 'My goods are beyond price.' Now, these men had secretly found out that there was no cargo of his aboard the ship. So they laughed and accused him of pretending to be wealthy when he was clearly poor.

Suddenly pirates swarmed all over the deck. Each was armed with a sword and dagger. With fearsome shouts they ordered the crew to lay down their weapons. They took the ship without a fight. The valuable cargo was seized at once. Next, the passengers were robbed of their jewellery and fine clothes. The stranger was left untouched, for his clothes were not worth stealing. Then the pirates sailed both ships to a faraway land. There they allowed the passengers and crew to row ashore to a small port.

Someone on the dockside recognized the stranger. 'This man is world-famous for

his learning,' he announced. He took the professor to the town hall where the mayor greeted him warmly and arranged a comfortable lodging. Later he persuaded the scholar to deliver a series of lectures. Large numbers flocked to listen. They were rewarded by fascinating talks on a wide variety of topics. With the money he received for his lectures the professor set up house and in a short time became an important figure in the town.

Meanwhile the merchants were finding it hard to keep body and soul together. They were tradesmen who had nothing to sell. Being penniless, they could not set themselves up in business. They had no other skills by which to earn a living. Employers had no use for untrained strangers dressed in undershirts. The merchants faced a bleak, hungry future.

Then they heard of the professor's good fortune. Swallowing their pride they went and asked him for help. He swiftly found jobs for all of them. He reminded them of his claim that his goods were beyond price. Knowledge, he explained, is a kind of wealth that cannot be bought or sold: it must be earned by hard study. And it cannot be stolen, even by pirates!

The Converted Snake

(Adapted from a story by *Sri Ramakrishna*)

A holy man was walking along a country road when a snake glided out from under a rock and headed straight for him. Its forked tongue flickered in and out and its dark eyes glittered with hate. The priest stopped. Not a trace of fear showed on his face as he spoke: 'Brother Snake, the people who live around here have told me all about you. You attack passers-by who mean you no harm – indeed, who are dead scared of you – and injure them, often seriously. Now I want you to listen to me while I tell you what I think of your behaviour.'

For ten minutes he addressed the astonished snake. Making war on humans was all wrong, he said. Most creatures killed for food, but there was no possibility of a snake being able to eat a man. All the great teachers of the past had urged us to be kind to each other. If we injure others they will strike back, thus starting a series of tit-for-tat attacks in which both parties are hurt. It was true that humans are often cruel, but that was no reason for behaving like them.

The snake listened to all this without moving or saying a word. Then he said, 'You're right. It's wicked to harm innocent people. I promise I'll stop it right now. From this day on no man, woman or child has anything to fear from me.' He was so plainly sincere that the holy man was delighted. He assured the snake that he had made a wise decision he would never regret.

Not long afterwards the priest happened to be passing by the same place. He was shocked to see the snake lying bruised and battered under the rock. One eye was closed and swollen. 'In heaven's name what happened to you?' exclaimed the man.

'I took your advice,' groaned the snake. 'I stopped attacking humans. Soon every-body knew I was harmless so they've been coming here – even small kids – and kicking the daylights out of me ever since.'

The holy man was silent for a time. 'My dear fellow, perhaps I'm partly to blame. I should have warned you that this would happen. Sad to say, there are some folk who cannot resist hurting anyone who will not hit back. You must let it be known that if you are attacked you will strike back. By all means don't deliver the first blow, but don't let anyone injure you. Try to scare troublemakers away by hissing at them in your most frightening manner.'

Shedding the Bracelets

(Adapted from *The Tso-ch'an San-mei Ching*)

The king, lying face down on his silk bedspread, frowned at the maddening noise. Tinkle, tinkle. He had lain down to get away from the sweaty heat of the burning afternoon and from all the worries of his high position. At each side of the jewelled bed knelt a slave-girl, cooling her lord with slow movements of a feathered fan. Another servant sat on the bed rubbing ointment on to his bare shoulders. This should have soothed him as it had in the past, but today was different. You see, one girl was wearing a cluster of bracelets on her wrists, as Indian girls do, and when she moved her arms they jangled. It was not a loud noise, but enough to disturb the king, who wanted only to close his eyes and feel the welcome breeze from the fans and expert hands coaxing the weariness from his body.

Tinkle, tinkle.

'The king murmured to himself, 'This can't go on.' Gently he spoke to the girl. 'Child, would you mind taking off one of your bangles. The noise, you know . . .'

Blushing, the servant quickly took one off. The king gratefully closed his eyes and prepared to doze off. He hoped he would manage to sleep. He deeply longed to forget the cares that rulers must face – making good laws, choosing wise minis-

ters, settling quarrels among his people. He also wished to close his mind to his temptations, for in those days kings were powerful enough to do anything they liked. They could be – and often were – cruel and lazy.

Tinkle, tinkle. The bracelets brought the dozing man back fully awake. This time he spoke in a sharper tone. 'My dear, the noise still bothers me. Would you be so good as to take another bangle off?'

Swiftly the girl obeyed. For some minutes there was silence and the king settled himself again for sleep. Then the bracelets tinkled – more quietly, but enough to make the great man groan. Politely he asked the slave-girl to remove another bangle. She did so. Shortly afterwards the remaining trinkets gave a musical rattle.

'Another please,' said the king.

The girl obeyed but it was no good. The noise went on. The king made her carry on taking them off until there was only one left. The jangling grew fainter as she shed the bracelets and stopped when she reached the last.

Thankfully the king closed his eyes. Surely sleep would come now. But it did not. A few moments later he opened his eyes again. He had just had a remarkable, exciting thought. Just as the girl had reduced the noise by taking off her bangles so he would get rid of his worries by giving up his kingdom. He would find peace of mind by shedding his throne, wealth, ministers, people and all wordly wants. The pleasures of being a king were like the girl's bracelets; they looked attractive but would not let one rest.

That very day he left the palace. He became poor and spent his time studying his religion far from the court. He found peace. Some said he had acted wisely in giving up his problems but others disagreed. They thought he should have stayed to face his worries like everyone else. He took the easy way out, they scoffed. What do you think?

POEMS

Against Quarrelling and Fighting

By Isaac Watts

Let dogs delight to bark and bite,
  For God has made them so;
Let bears and lions growl and fight,
  For 'tis their nature too.

But children, you should never let
  Such angry passion rise;
Your little hands were never made
  To tear each others' eyes.

Whatever brawls disturb the street,
  There should be peace at home;
Where sisters dwell and brothers meet,
  Quarrels should never come.

Birds in their little nests agree;
  And 'tis a shameful sight,
When children of one family
  Fall out, and chide and fight.

The Bells of Heaven

By Ralph Hodgson

'Twould ring the bells of Heaven
The wildest peal for years,
If Parson lost his senses
And people came to theirs,
And he and they together
Knelt down with angry prayers
For tamed and shabby tigers
And dancing dogs and bears,
And wretched, blind pit ponies,
And little hunted hares.

Timothy Winters

By Charles Causley

Timothy Winters comes to school
With eyes as wide as a football-pool,
Ears like bombs and teeth like splinters:
A blitz of a boy is Timothy Winters.

His belly is white, his neck is dark,·
And his hair is an exclamation-mark.
His clothes are enough to scare a crow
And through his britches the blue winds
    blow.

When teacher talks he won't hear a word
And he shoots down dead the arithmetic-
    bird,
He licks the patterns off his plate
And he's not even heard of the Welfare
    State.

Timothy Winters has bloody feet
And he lives in a house on Suez Street,
He sleeps in a sack on the kitchen floor
And they say there aren't boys like him
    any more.

Old Man Winters likes his beer
And his missus ran off with a bombadier,
Grandma sits in the grate with a gin
And Timothy's dosed with an aspirin.

The Welfare Worker lies awake
But the law's as tricky as a ten-foot snake,
So Timothy Winters drinks his cup
And slowly goes on growing up.

At Morning Prayers the Headmaster
    helves*
For children less fortunate than ourselves,
And the loudest response in the room is
    when
Timothy Winters roars 'Amen!'

So come one angel, come on ten:
Timothy Winters says, 'Amen
Amen amen amen amen
Timothy Winters, Lord.'

                                    Amen.

*helves: pleads

Hate

By David Eva (aged 13)

Hate swelled up inside me,
Choking me, strangling me,
Hiding me from myself behind it.
I could only stand and watch me as I
    bellowed and shouted at my friend.

I heard me abuse him,
Poison others against him
And do many despicable things.
Then myself forced its way through
And I shook hands and said I was sorry.

Hate is a funny thing;
It splits you in two,
One part against the other,
So that you can never win.

Calchas Mourns the Death of Ajax

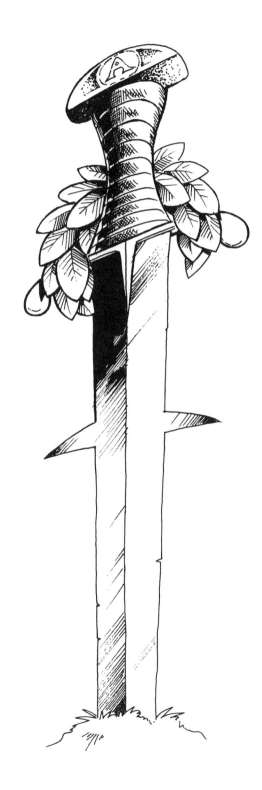

By James Shirley

The glories of our blood and state
   Are shadows, not substantial things;
There is no armour against fate;
   Death lays his icy hand on kings:
      Scepter and crown
      Must tumble down,
And in the dust be equal made
With the poor crooked scythe and spade.

Some men with swords may reap the field,
   And plant fresh laurels where they kill;
But their strong nerves at last must yield;
   They tame but one another still:
      Early or late,
      They stoop to fate,
And must give up their murmuring
breath,
When they, pale captives, creep to death.

The garlands wither on your brow,
   Then boast no more your mighty deeds;
Upon Death's purple altar now,
   See, where the victor–victim bleeds:
      Your heads must come
      To the cold tomb,
Only the actions of the just
Smell sweet, and blossom in their dust.

The Donkey

By G. K. Chesterton

When fishes flew and forests walked
And figs grew upon thorn,
Some moment when the moon was blood
Then surely I was born;

With monstrous head and sickening cry
And ears like errant wings,
The devil's walking parody
On all four-footed things.

The tattered outlaw of the earth,
Of ancient, crooked will;
Starve, scourge, deride me; I am dumb,
I keep my secret still.

Fools! For I also had my hour;
One far fierce hour and sweet:
There was a shout about my ears,
And palms before my feet.

King David and King Solomon

By J. B. Naylor

King David and King Solomon
    Led merry, merry lives,
With many, many lady friends
    And many, many wives;
But when old age crept over them,
    With many, many qualms,
King Solomon wrote the Proverbs,
    And King David wrote the Psalms.

96

I Am

By Ella Wheeler Wilcox

I know not whence I came,
   I know not whither I go;
But the fact stands clear that I am here
   In this world of pleasure and woe.
And out of the mist and murk
   Another truth stands plain:
It is in my power, each day and hour,
   To add to its joy or pain.

I know that the earth exists,
   It is none of my business why;
I cannot find out what it's all about,
   I would but waste time to try.
My life is a brief, brief thing,
   I am here for a little space;
And while I stay I would like, if I may,
   To brighten and better the place.

The trouble, I think, with us all
   Is the lack of a high conceit.
If each man thought he was sent to this
     spot
   To make it a bit more sweet
How soon we could gladden the world,
   How easily right all wrong,
If nobody shirked, and each one worked
   To help his fellows along!

Cease wondering why you came,
   Stop looking for faults and flaws;
Rise up today in your pride and say:
   'I am part of the First Great Cause!
However full the world,
   There is room for an earnest man.
It had need of me, or I would not be:
   I am here to strengthen the plan.'

The Camel's Hump

By Rudyard Kipling

The camel's hump is an ugly lump
   Which well you may see at the Zoo;
But uglier yet is the hump we get
   From having too little to do.

Kiddies and grown-ups too –oo –oo,
   If we haven't enough to do –oo –oo,
   We get the hump —
   Cameelious hump—
The hump that is black and blue!

We climb out of bed with a frouzly head
   And a snarly-yarly voice.
We shiver and scowl and we grunt and we
  growl
   At our bath and our boots and our toys;

And there ought to be a corner for me
   (And I know there is one for you)
   When we get the hump —
   Cameelious hump —
The hump that is black and blue!

The cure for this ill is not to sit still,
Or frowst with a book by the fire;
But to take a large hoe and a shovel also,
And dig till you gently perspire;

And then you'll find that the sun and the
  wind,
And the Djinn of the Garden too,
   Have lifted the hump —
   The horrible hump —
The hump that is black and blue!

I get it as well as you –oo –oo
If I haven't enough to do –oo –oo!
   We all get the hump —
   Cameelious hump —
Kiddies and grown-ups too!

FICTION

Of the Conquests and Charity of Our Lord

(Adapted from *The Gesta Romanorum*)

The priestess sat upright on her three-legged golden chair. Her eyes were closed and she gave no sign of being aware of the man who knelt before her. 'Great priestess,' he began, 'I have been sent by my master Codrus, king of Athens. He speaks highly of your power to see what is hidden in the future. Apollo, god of prophecy, speaks through your lips. My master commands me to ask you a question.'

The priestess whispered: 'Ask.'

'The Dorians are marching to attack Athens. To protect the city Codrus must give battle soon. The question is: who will win the battle?'

A long silence followed. The priestess sat still, breathing heavily like one in a deep sleep. At last she murmured, 'The field will be won by the army whose chief will be killed by the enemy.'

The servant, unsure if he had heard her words aright, stammered: 'Surely, surely you mean that the field will be won by the army that kills the enemy chief.'

'No,' came the reply, 'the victors will lose their leader.'

When Codrus heard this forecast he knew that he must die to save his city. When the day of battle came he donned his crown and kingly armour. Mounted on a horse whose rich trappings caught every eye, he led his army towards the foe. At the head of his men he plunged into the fray. Time and again he was at the mercy of the enemy but each time his attacker put up his sword and ran away.

Finally Codrus understood. The Dorians too had heard of the prophecy and were under strict orders not to kill the king. Swiftly he changed clothes with a slave. Then he hurled himself into the battle where the struggle was most fierce. The Dorians, deceived by his tattered tunic and sandals, surrounded him and cut him down. The men of Athens, enraged by the death of their king, swept the enemy from the field. The city was saved.

Christians of olden times told this story in praise of Jesus. Like Codrus he too had taken on the role of a servant, they said. As the king had welcomed death to preserve Athens, so Jesus had given his life for all mankind.

How the Chimney-sweep got the Ear of the Emperor

(Adapted from a story by Mark Twain)

Disease, like a river in flood, swept through the army. Strong men lay groaning on their camp beds, weak as day-old chicks. The emperor grew alarmed. He grew even more alarmed when he himself was struck down with the dread disorder. The court doctors scurried to his bedside. The oldest and wisest, whom the emperor fondly called his Chief Assassin, stated: 'There is no cure for your illness. Only the strength of your body can make you well. We must wait patiently.' With that he emptied the contents of a chemist's shop into his royal lord and waited patiently for pay-day.

The news of the emperor's sickness flashed through the land. Everyone was shocked, and everyone claimed to know a cure. Even Jimmy, the little chimney-sweep, was sure he knew the answer. He told his friend Tommy, who worked on his father's dust-cart: 'I *must* get this information to the emperor.'

'But what's the cure?' asked Tommy.

'A slice of melon.'

Tommy doubled up and shook with laughter. Angrily his friend said, 'It's true. It works. That grey-headed coloured man told me, and he *knows*. I'm going to sit down right now and write to the palace —'

'Don't bother,' said Tommy. 'Every crackpot in the country is writing to the palace with a miracle cure. Your letter will never be read. Every day I cart away sackloads of unopened letters. No, you must use my plan to get to the ear of the emperor.'

'What's your plan?' asked Jimmy.

'Well, everybody in the world, high or low, has a special friend who would do anything for him. I'll go to my special friend the butcher and tell him about your slice of melon cure. I'll beg him to pass the news on to *his* great friend, the chestnut-seller. She in turn must tell her aunt, the greengrocer. The greengrocer will tell the police sergeant, who will tell the judge, who will tell the Lord Mayor —'

'Go on, you're getting close!' shouted Jimmy excitedly.

'— who will tell the Master of the Hounds, who will pass it on to the Lord High Chamberlain. It is he who will order the emperor's little servant-boy to take the great man a slice of melon.'

The plot worked. The very next night the servant-boy tiptoed into the sick man's bedchamber. He bore a dish on which rested a curved wedge of pink juicy melon. The emperor looked at the fruit with disgust, sighed, grumbled, but finally ate it.

He awoke in the morning feeling as light and airy as a Tipperary rag-man. Spring-ing from his bed he summoned his servant and asked him where he had heard of the melon cure. 'The Lord High Chamberlain,' the boy replied.

'I shall reward him richly,' cried his delighted master. 'He will be made a duke, and I shall give him a vast estate taken from someone I do not like.'

When the Lord High Chamberlain heard this news he hurried to the emperor and confessed that the Master of the Hounds had told him of the melon remedy. 'Then it is he who will receive my thanks,' said the monarch. 'I shall give him slightly less than I intended to give you, for he is a little lower in rank. It is my pleasure that he be made a lord, with a large income paid from the nation's taxes.'

The Master of Hounds, being an honest fellow, said that the cure was not his, but the Lord Mayor's. The emperor then sent for his Grand High Chief Detective. He instructed him to trace the cure back to the person who had first suggested it. That person must be suitably rewarded, he insisted.

Next day the Grand High Chief Detective reported that he had followed the trail of the cure back to Jimmy the chimney-sweep. 'That boy saved my life,' said the emperor gratefully, 'and he shall not regret it.' The Lord High Chamberlain was ordered to send Jimmy a pair of the emperor's second-best boots. Unfortunately they were too big for the little chimney-sweep. He gave them to the old coloured man. They fitted him very well so I suppose everything turned out fine in the end.

The Necklace

(Adapted from the story by *Guy de Maupassant*)

Madame Loisel, the pretty young wife of a government clerk, was dissatisfied with her life. Her little home, tended by a single kitchen-maid, fell far short of her secret dreams. She longed to live in an elegant mansion, attended by grave footmen in knee-breeches. She saw herself as a charming hostess entertaining men and women of importance in silken drawing-rooms.

One evening her husband brought home a printed card. It was an invitation to a party to be given by his minister. All the top officials and their wives would be there. To his surprise Madame Loisel declared that she would not go. None of her dresses was fashionable enough. Her husband offered to buy her a new one and she gladly accepted. She bought a handsome gown that fitted her perfectly. Then she remembered that she had no jewellery. The thought of mingling with glittering ladies plunged her into fresh misery. Her husband suggested that she borrow a piece from a friend of her schooldays, Madame Forestier. Next day she visited her friend and made her request. Madame Forestier fetched her jewel-box and told her to take anything she fancied. She chose a necklace of finely cut transparent stones.

The party was a triumph for Madame Loisel. The most attractive woman in the room, she was besieged by admiring young men eager to lead her on to the dance floor for the next waltz. Her heart sang and her smile was no less radiant than the necklace at her throat. It was almost dawn before she unwillingly left.

When she looked at herself in the bedroom mirror she uttered a horrified cry. The necklace was missing. A frantic search of the house was in vain. Her husband went out and retraced their route to the party but without success. During the next week he took every possible step to recover the jewellery but his efforts were useless. They were forced to face the fact that the necklace was lost for good.

Madame Loisel could not face telling her friend of the disaster. She and her husband went from one jeweller to another, desperately seeking an exact replica of the missing piece. At last they found it. The price was thirty-six thousand francs – a huge sum for a humble office-worker. Loisel raised it by clearing out his bank account and borrowing the rest from friends and money-lenders. Madame Loisel took the diamond necklace to her friend, trembling lest she should notice the substitution. To her vast relief Madame Forestier did not.

To pay their debts the unhappy couple dismissed the kitchen-maid and moved to a cheap top-floor flat. Loisel brought in a little extra money by working at tradesmen's accounts in the evenings. For the first time his wife scrubbed, swept and shopped. They ate only the simplest food in order to save every sou. When ten years had passed they had paid all their debts.

One Sunday, while strolling in the park,

Madame Loisel saw Madame Forestier approaching. She greeted her. At first her friend did not recognize the pale, wrinkled and shabby woman who stood before her. Then, when Madame Loisel declared herself, she could not help exclaiming: 'How you have changed!' The clerk's wife then told the whole story of the lost necklace, of replacing it with a similar string of diamonds and of their struggle to repay their debts. 'And you never noticed the difference,' she finished, smiling.

Madame Forestier's face was lined with distress. 'You bought a *diamond* necklace to replace mine!' she cried. 'But mine was imitation – worth only a few francs.'

Why the Negro is Black

(Adapted from the story by Joel Chandler Harris)

Uncle Remus, the coloured storyteller, was making shoelaces. The little boy who was watching him noticed that the palms of his hands were as white as his own. He asked the reason for this, hoping that the old man would reply with a good story. He was not disappointed.

Far back in the old days, Uncle Remus told him, *everyone* was black. The English, the Chinese, the Eskimos – all were as dark-skinned as Africans. There were no people of any other colour. Then there came news of a magic pond. It was said that anyone who bathed in its waters would come out white-skinned. Most people laughed at the story. It was just a fairy tale, they scoffed. There was no such pond. One man set out to find it. When he returned to his family they thought their eyes were playing tricks. His skin was as pale as a summer cloud.

All of a sudden everybody wanted to be white! Thousands rushed headlong towards the pond. The quickest runners plunged in first. They emerged as white men, delighted with their newly bleached skin. Others dived in after them, with the same result. Soon the pool was alive with laughing palefaces. Crowds pushed and

struggled on its banks, eager to jump in. Before long the level of water had sunk, for everyone used up a little. A short while later it was no deeper than a fish-tank. Latecomers could only scoop up handfuls and splash themselves. They came out with pale yellow skins and went off to live in China.

At last there was no water left. Those who had come last walked barefoot on the wet bed of the pond. They bent down and pressed their palms on the damp earth. Then, still dark-skinned, they set out for their home in Africa. Only the soles of their feet and the palms of their hands were white.

That is why some men are black, Uncle Remus told the little boy. It is a charming story but is not really true. We now know that colouring matter in the skin gives Negroes their dark complexion. This helps them to withstand the effects of the hot African sun. Inside their skin they are just like everybody else.

The Acharnians

(Adapted from the play by Aristophanes)

Long ago the city of Athens embarked on a long and bloody war. Together with several friendly cities she fought Sparta and her allies. The war brought famine and plague – a plague that carried off thousands, including the Athenian leader, Pericles.

One day an old farmer named Dikaeopolis, who had been ordered into the city to do sentry duty, announced that he had had enough of the madness of war. Every wise man since the beginning of time had raised his voice against it. He would no longer lift a finger against the enemies of Athens. Furthermore he intended to sign a separate peace with them. With that he signed and dispatched a peace treaty to Sparta, to the horror of his fellow-citizens.

The people of Acharnae were particularly enraged. Their town had suffered badly at the hands of the enemy. A number of their leading citizens surrounded Dikaeopolis and declared their intention of stoning him to death. He was a traitor, they shouted, who was denying his duty to the state.

Dikaeopolis persuaded them to let him make one speech in defence of his action, confident that his quick brain and blistering tongue would save his life. He began

by stating that he had no grudge against the enemy, who were starving and dying just like themselves. The first act of the war, he reminded them, had been the theft by two young Athenians of a girl from Megara. So they must not forget that Athens herself had triggered the conflict. Furious, the Megarians had carried off two girls from Athens. All three girls were delighted to be whisked off by strapping young men but the two cities bristled with offended pride. Athenian customs officials seized cargoes of Megarian jackets and sold them privately, lining their own pockets. Megara appealed to her friends for help. Athens enlisted her allies. The tragedy began.

So he would not take up arms, Dikaeopolis told the Acharnians, just because a few touchy leaders on both sides felt they had been insulted. That was no reason to send thousands of blameless soldiers to an early grave. Such leaders should be disobeyed. Blockheads like those would declare war if someone stole a mangy dog.

This speech, delivered with many a joke and jibe, completely won over his audience. Every word seemed clear common sense to the Acharnians. Then along came General Lamachos, a splendid figure in gleaming armour and plumed helmet. Bitterly he accused Dikaeopolis of treason.

The old farmer replied with equal hostility. War was a lovely job for generals, he snarled. They pranced about in fancy uniforms, full of fresh hope of extra pay and promotion. They preened themselves like actors, prated about the glory of laying down one's life for freedom and snapped out orders at a safe distance from the actual fighting. But war was misery and horror for everyone else. He knew what he was talking about, claimed Dikaeopolis, for he had fought in the ranks as a plain private.

Lamachos, speechless with rage, rushed off, tripping over his sword as he went. Dikaeopolis lived out the war at peace with the Spartans. He traded freely with them, exchanging foodstuffs which both parties desperately needed. When Lamachos returned from the fighting, wounded – he had fallen in a ditch and sprained his ankle – he found the old farmer living like a lord among his starving neighbours. Dikaeopolis had grown plump and merry on a diet of honey, cheese and foreign wine. He was a living reproach to war-makers.

A Little Pilgrim

(Adapted from a story by Stephen Crane)

'Children, be kind,' urged the Sunday School teacher. 'You have all been saddened – as I have – by the news of the terrible earthquake at Charleston. Let us help our fellow-Americans who suffered in it. I suggest that we do without a Christmas tree this year. Let us send the money we would have spent on it to the homeless victims. All those in favour, please raise your hands.'

Every hand rose. Even Jimmie Trescott, who was stunned by the loss of the tree, managed to raise an unwilling arm. In his mind's eye he recalled the scene last Christmas. Coloured candles, flickering among its branches, turned the tree into a pyramid of light. Ribboned parcels nestled among the spiny leaves. A ring of young faces, flushed with the magic of Christmas, gazed upward in silent awe. Sighing, Jimmie rose and made his way home with a heavy heart.

A few days later he said to his father, 'Pa, is it all right if I change Sunday schools? I'd like to start going to the one at the Big Progressive Church.'

His father, an easy-going doctor, looked surprised. 'Why? What's wrong with the Presbyterian Church School?'

'Well, er, um,' said Jimmie, 'some of the boys there are a bit rough.' He thought it

best not to mention that he had learned that the Big Progressives always had a Christmas tree.

'I guess that'll be okay, son,' said Dr Trescott mildly. 'After all, both churches worship the same God. Both teach the value of the Christian way of life.'

On the following Sunday afternoon Jimmie took his seat in his new church school. He was ill at ease. Most of the other children were unknown to him. The teacher, a young woman who wore thick spectacles and a deeply religious expression, made him feel nervous. He did not know the tune of the hymn 'Pull for the shore, sailor, Pull for the Shore', and was obliged to open and close his mouth in a noiseless bluff.

A bad moment came during the Lesson. The teacher asked him what 'the temple of the Lord' meant. Every eye was on Jimmie. He blushed and mumbled, 'I dunno.' A boy in the front pew cried, 'It means church, same as this.'

'Well done, Clarence,' said the teacher. 'You always know the answer.'

Jimmie stared at the back of the boy's head with a look that showed no trace of Christian kindness. Clarence, he decided, was one of those know-all kids who make life hell for all the rest. He looked away and his gaze fell on a large picture of the Martyrdom of St Stephen. White-robed men, their faces twisted with hate, hurled rocks at the doomed saint. Bleeding from many wounds, he raised his eyes to Heaven in a kind of tortured joy. Jimmie quickly imagined Clarence in St Stephen's place. A wicked little smile played around the corners of his mouth.

He was wrenched from his daydream by the voice of the teacher. '— so I suggest we do without the Christmas tree and send the money to the homeless sufferers. All those in favour?'

Every hand rose.

The True Enjoyments of Life

(Adapted from a story by Thomas Percival)

As the prison doors boomed shut behind him the old Chinaman narrowed his eyes against the glare of the sun. Fifty years had passed since he last stood in the open air. Now the new emperor had passed a law freeing all those imprisoned for debt. The old man, Wang Lo, was suddenly plucked from the dank gloom of his underground cell to the brightness of a summer morning.

Joy welled up in his soul as he gazed on a world whose beauty he had almost forgotten. The sun, still masked by the dawn mist, cast a tender glow over the countryside. Distant peaks added a touch of majesty. Curved fields and flowing hills capped by trees of darker green delighted the eye. The air, fresh as spring water, was filled with the small sounds of summer.

So entranced was Wang Lo by the magic of the scene that it was some time before he forced himself to think of the future. He must hasten to Peking, he told himself. With the eye of memory he pictured the old city of his birth, ringed by mountains, proudly displaying its superb palaces and pagodas. There he would clasp again all those most dear to him. There he would bask in the love of his family and friends for his remaining years. Wrapping his cloak about his shoulders he hurried away from the prison with all the speed his ancient legs could muster.

A week later Wang Lo threw himself at the emperor's feet and begged: 'For pity's sake send me back to my cell.'

The great man's attendants looked thunderstruck. The emperor, who had been trained from childhood to hide his feelings, gaped at Wang Lo in amazement. 'Do you know what you are saying?' he demanded. 'Are you really asking me to throw you back into that filthy prison?'

'I am.'

The emperor stared at the old man. 'But why should you cast away your freedom? Surely your release from prison brought you happiness?'

'Happiness,' said Wang Lo, 'is a feeble word to describe the joy I felt when I stepped out into the world. I thought I should burst with ecstasy. I hurried off to my home city marvelling at the beauties of Nature and the cheerful faces of my fellow-men. As I passed the Temple of Confucius I met an old beggar whose face I knew. We had been boyhood friends. "How is my wife?" I asked eagerly.

'His welcoming smile vanished. He tried to speak but the words wouldn't come. Silently he pointed to the graveyard. I felt as if someone had torn my heart out. When I found my voice I said, "And my sons? What about my boys?"

'"Scattered to the four winds. No one has seen or heard of them these thirty years."

'Suddenly I was alone – alone in a city of happy strangers. For the first time I felt the full force of the old curse "May you outlive your family and friends." All at once I longed to be back in my cell. No one would see my misery there. I should be spared the torture of watching others enjoy the kind of full rich life which I had lost forever. No longer should I feel like a man dying of thirst, though surrounded by cool streams.'

When Wang Lo finished his story there was a long stillness. Then the emperor sadly ordered that he be taken back to prison.

Riquet of the Tuft

(Adapted from a story by Charles Perrault)

The queen of a distant land gave birth to a baby boy. He was so ugly and ill-shaped that she burst into tears. A fairy who was present said, 'Lady, do not be so sad. Your son will not be handsome but he will be gifted in other ways. He will be clever and witty. He will also possess the strange power to make the woman he loves just as clever as himself.' The little boy had a curious tuft of long hair above his forehead so he became known as Riquet of the Tuft.

Seven years later the queen of another country had a baby girl. The child was so beautiful that the queen was beside herself with joy. The fairy who had been present at Riquet's birth said, 'Lady, your daughter will grow up to be the loveliest girl in the land, but she will also be the most stupid. However, she will have the magic gift of being able to make the man she loves as good-looking as herself.'

The fairy was right. The princess grew up to be so lovely that strangers stood amazed when they first saw her. But after talking to her for a few minutes they drifted away, bored by her silly talk and empty mind. She was sharply aware of her dullness and became more unhappy every day.

While walking in the woods one day she met a remarkably ugly young man. He told her he was Riquet of the Tuft. 'The moment I clapped eyes on your portrait I fell in love with you,' he said, 'and I made up my mind to ask you to marry me.'

'No one could love someone as stupid as I,' the princess answered. Riquet's bright wit and quick tongue had charmed her but she was offended by his big red nose and crooked body.

'I truly love you,' said Riquet, 'and I shall give you a year to make up your mind whether to marry me or not. As for your stupidity, I now use my magic power to make you as clever as myself.'

Suddenly the fogs rolled away from the girl's brain. Fresh, exciting thoughts swarmed in her head and she was no longer tongue-tied. She ran back to the palace to tell her father the wonderful news. He soon let the whole world know that his daughter was not only beautiful but brainy. Shortly afterwards princes from all parts, bewitched by her new-found brilliance, were asking for her hand in marriage. Her father told her she must choose one of them in the near future. She had forgotten Riquet. He had asked her to marry him in the last moments of her stupidity, when her memory was poor.

One day the princess went for a walk in the woods. A rumbling noise from under the ground startled her. Then the earth opened up to disclose a wide dining-hall below. Cooks and kitchen-maids scurried around carrying plates of food. A whole pig revolved lazily over a huge log fire. Long tables draped in snowy linen shimmered with gold plate and jewelled goblets. The princess asked a cook what was going on. 'Riquet of the Tuft is to be married to the princess tomorrow,' he replied.

In that instant the girl remembered her meeting with Riquet a year before. She turned to go. Riquet stood in her path. There and then the happy princess agreed to marry him. 'You changed me by your power,' she said, 'and now I'll change you by mine.' Straight away the ugly little fellow became as handsome as his bride was lovely.

Mind you, some people claimed that she only *thought* that Riquet was beautiful. Love, they said, is itself a kind of magic that enables us to see others as they *are*, not as they look.

The Bottle-Imp

(Adapted from a story by Johann Musaus)

A young man named Richard spent all his money in a whirl of foolish pleasures. Then he met a soldier who told him a weird tale. He had in his possession a bottle in which a small black devil lived. This bottle-imp could grant any wish of its owner. The bottle could be sold only for less than the owner had paid for it. The last person to possess it would belong to Lucifer, the chief devil, and his soul would go to Hell.

Thrilled by the hope of riches, Richard gave the soldier five ducats and took the bottle. Inside the dark glass a tiny figure flickered and jumped. An eerie mist, whose colour changed constantly, swirled around it, making it impossible to see the creature clearly. The greedy young man at once demanded ten ducats. They suddenly appeared in his hand. Joyously Richard went off, promising himself all the luxuries life could provide. He kept that promise. Splendid mansions richly furnished, costly garments, food and drink fit for a king – he obtained them merely by wishing for them. Every day became more delightful than the one before.

Slowly a change crept over him. His grand possessions no longer pleased him. He ceased gathering the world's great prizes, for the thrill of owning them had withered. Fear of Hell grew in his soul.

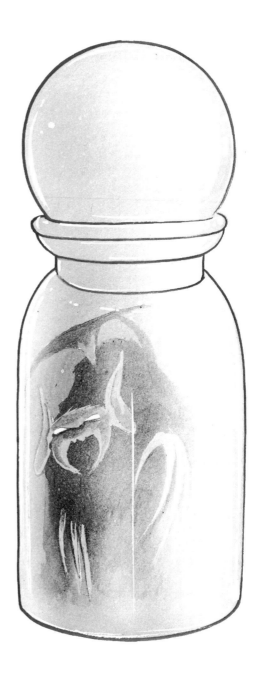

The thought that he might not be able to sell the bottle filled him with terror. After all, he had bought it for just five ducats. Who would buy it for less? He offered the bottle to his doctor for three ducats without telling him of the devil's bargain. To his huge relief the doctor bought it.

Richard's peace of mind did not last long. The doctor, on finding out how dangerous the bottle was, tricked the young man into buying it back for two ducats. Richard was again struck with dread. How could he sell it for a single ducat?

In panic he set off for India where two princes were at war. He joined one of their armies and tried to get rid of the deadly vessel. He sold it to a soldier but bought it back by accident. Several times more he managed to sell it but each time, by chance or trickery, the bottle found its way back to him. His last purchase of it cost him a single heller, the smallest coin in the land. His soul was flooded with despair. It now seemed impossible to dispose of the bottle, and he faced everlasting pain.

Then he met a giant horseman dressed in blood-red. This man offered to buy the bottle. But how could he do that, asked Richard, since there was no coin smaller than a heller? The strange horseman, who claimed magic powers, told him exactly what he must do.

Next morning Richard was riding through a deep valley when he saw a horned monster attacking a richly-dressed young man. He spurred his horse to the scene and drove the animal off with his club. The young man revealed that he was the prince of that country and declared that he was so grateful to Richard for saving his life that he would give him anything he asked. Richard begged him to create a new coin, the half-heller, and to give him just two. Laughing, the prince agreed. The coins were quickly minted. Richard took two and rushed off to meet the horseman. He gave him the coins. Then he handed over the bottle and the stranger gave him in exchange one half-heller, the smallest coin in the world.

As soon as the evil glass left his fingers an immense peace filled Richard's mind. He was free! To the end of his life he remembered that wonderful moment. He often told the whole story to his grandchildren. It should serve as a terrible warning to them, he said. A craving for great possessions is like a bottle-imp that drags us to disaster.

Patriots

(Adapted from Goldsmith)

'I've never been so worried,' the Englishman said. 'The French are ready to invade our country and take it over. And you know what that means? They'll take away our freedom. After all, they themselves are slaves so it stands to reason that they won't let us be free.' He spoke angrily through the barred window of his prison cell to the two men outside. One was a porter who carried heavy loads across eighteenth-century London. He had stopped for a rest outside the prison. The other was a soldier standing at a window across the narrow street.

'You've hit the nail on the head,' said the porter. 'The French are slaves. There can be no doubt about it. They're fit only —' He stopped, searching about in his mind for the nastiest insult he could find. 'They're fit only to carry burdens.' He looked from one man to the other as if defying them to disagree with him.

The soldier raised a tumbler to his lips and took a long swig of the strong spirits it contained. 'They would take away our religion,' he roared, 'the sacred religion which directs our lives. May the devil sink me in flames if I'll let that happen.' And he continued drinking and swearing at the top of his lungs.

A passing Chinaman who overheard the three men's conversation was amazed. What an inscrutable race these English are, he thought. Their convicts boast of their freedom, their porters despise those who carry burdens, and the ruffians prattle about their best of all religions.

The Hardest Task

(Adapted from a story by David Lamond)

'Have you ever seen anything half so lovely in all your life?'

The speaker was Baron Ashmead, lord of Castle Ashmead and the broad fields that encircled it. He stood in the middle of his famous rose-garden with his Scottish friend, the Laird of Glenbeg. 'I truly believe my flowers are the finest in the world,' the baron went on. 'Just look at my ramblers, my wild roses, my climbers, my dwarf bushes.'

The laird looked around in silent wonder. The wide garden, bounded by hedges decked with sweet briar and dog roses, was a coloured and scented delight. As the eye visited each bloom – yellow, crimson, white or pink – it seemed more beautiful than all the others. The Scot was enchanted by the scene but secretly amused at his friend. The way the baron spoke of *my* ramblers, *my* wild roses, *my* garden, seemed to him a little out of place. After all, the man had not lifted a finger (or a spade) to help the flowers grow.

A sudden cry of rage made him jump. The baron was glaring at a puffy red rose, his eyes bulging with horror. The heart of the bloom was missing – eaten by an insect. In a voice that shook with fury Baron Ashmead yelled for his steward. He ordered him to sack the head-gardener at once. 'The fool has allowed a garden pest to ruin this flower,' he bellowed. 'Get him off my land right now and tell him never to return. Give his job to the under-gardener.'

Next morning the under-gardener took up his new duties. Soon the results were there for all to see. Weeds ranged over the rose-beds like an ever-spreading carpet. They curled up the stems in tangled spirals. Diseases struck the frail petals, leaving them black and withered. The garden, so recently a sweet-smelling joy, became a wilderness. The under-gardener lost his job and was replaced by a new man. He was no better. The baron gave up walking in his shabby rose-garden. Visitors who asked to see it were put off with lame excuses. The weather was bad for roses, he would stammer. Or the sun was too strong.

One day Baron Ashmead was riding through the marketplace with his steward. He happened to glance at a flower stall. Among the blossoms there nestled a bunch of roses, every one a flawless beauty. The baron turned to his steward. 'Find the man who grew those blooms,' he ordered. 'Tell him I'll pay him twenty crowns a year to work for me.' The servant rushed off and quickly tracked down the grower. You do not need to be a genius to guess who it was. Yes, it was the baron's old gardener, Seth by name. When the steward told him of his master's offer he spoke firmly: 'No, no, no, no, no.'

The baron was disappointed by Seth's reply but did not give up hope. 'Tell him I'll make it forty crowns,' he said. His steward delivered the new offer. Seth smiled. 'It's not the money,' he said. 'He treated me bad. If he's willing to tell me he's sorry I'll go back to my old job at my old wage. That's all I ask – a simple apology.'

'No, no, no, no, no,' was Baron Ashmead's response to this demand. 'I am an English nobleman and he is a common gardener. It is no more likely that I shall apologise than that men will fly to the moon.' However, he was sharply tempted to say the few words that would bring Seth back. In his inner eye he pictured the garden in all its one-time glory. He struggled with himself. Should he or shouldn't he? He wrote to the Laird of Glenbeg telling him of his problem.

Back came the reply: 'My dear old friend, I strongly advise you to apologise.

You did behave badly. It is true that the garden is yours in the eyes of the law. But ask yourself this: who dug it, weeded it, watered it, pruned it, carried out the hundred and one chores that made it such a marvel? A proud man's hardest task is to say he is sorry. I know you are generous enough to do so.'

'I humbly ask your forgiveness,' said the baron to Seth next day. 'Please, please come back to my garden.' Seth picked up his tools and was hard at work within an hour. Six months later the rose-garden was bright with perfect blooms. When the laird arrived on a visit he asked his host to show him around it. The baron sent for Seth. Putting his arm around the gardener's shoulders he said, 'Seth and I will show you. *We* are prouder than ever of *our* roses.'

Of Christ Who Died Innocent

(Adapted from the *Gesta Romanorum*)

In a certain city long ago knights were obliged by law to be buried in full armour. The law also ruled that anyone who stole the armour from the dead man should be put to death. Now it happened that soon after this order was made public a large army attacked the city. Spears and arrows rained down from all sides, killing hundreds. Every house became a place of mourning, for there was not one that had not lost a son or husband. The citizens were so gripped by fear that they could scarcely defend their walls. It seemed only a matter of time before the enemy crushed them.

Then a brave knight managed to make his way into the city. 'I have come to help you,' he told the besieged defenders, 'but I am unarmed, as you see.'

'You shall have armour,' said a captain. 'We buried a knight the other day. Take his battle-gear and save our city.'

The stranger dug up the grave and donned the dead man's armour. He took command of the citizen army, urging them to strive with all their strength to throw back the enemy. With new hope they manned their battle-stations. The enemy mounted attack after attack but were hurled back every time. Their assaults became more feeble as they gradually lost hope of capturing the city. Finally the defenders, led by the masterful knight, rode out of the city gates and put their foes to flight. The knight restored his armour to the dead man's grave, watched by a throng of grateful citizens.

Some men, jealous of the warrior's deeds, accused him before the judge of having plundered the grave. He defended himself stoutly. 'I had to choose between taking the armour or permitting a great slaughter. I chose the smaller crime. If one of the houses in your city caught fire you would drench it with water. That house would be ruined but all the other dwellings in the city would be saved. By breaking one law I saved all your laws, not to mention your *lives*.'

These words served only to enrage his enemies who yelled: 'Away with him, away with him!' Fearful of offending his fellow-citizens, the judge stated that the law must be put into force. He passed the death sentence. The knight was taken out and put to death by people who owed him their lives.

Preachers of olden times told this story to show how savagely Jesus was treated. Just as the knight arrived to rescue the city, so Jesus came to save the world. He too was sentenced by a feeble judge and killed by those he had laboured to serve.

FOLK STORIES

The Governor and the Christians

Diocletian, Emperor of Rome and lord of half the world, became alarmed as more and more of his subjects declared themselves Christians. He made up his mind to stamp out the new creed. He gave orders that all followers of Jesus were to be dismissed from the army and civil service. Churches must be knocked down and Christian books burnt. Any citizen who refused to sacrifice to the old Roman gods would be put to death.

These orders were carried out. Throughout Europe countless Christians suffered and died. Many went to their deaths bravely, eager to give up their lives for what they believed, as Jesus had done three hundred years before. Their actions were widely admired. People flocked to join them, convinced that a faith worth dying for was worth living for.

The governor of a Roman province decided to root out the infant faith by one artful ruse. On a bitterly cold winter's night he sent his guards to fetch twenty Christian prisoners from their cells. He announced to his captives: 'You shall all be taken to a frozen lake nearby. There you will be forced to stand all night on the ice. Naturally you will die if you do so, but I shall give you a chance to save yourselves. If at any time during the night you decide to give up this Christian nonsense you may hurry to the lakeside hut. There you will find food, drink and warm clothes. You will also find an army captain placed there to see that no one escapes. I am certain that none of you will die for your faith in the darkness and cold.'

The prisoners were led out by a tough captain, fully armed. Next morning the governor rode down to the lake to see the result of his cruel test. He was sure that the prisoners would have given in. He could then label all Christians as cowards.

From a distance he spied a lone figure standing outside the hut. On the ice sprawled twenty bodies, frozen in death. The governor scowled in fury and spurred his horse faster. When he reached the hut he was amazed to see that the man standing there was one of the prisoners. 'What's the meaning of this?' he demanded.

The man's face was haggard with shame. 'I couldn't go through with it,' he whispered. 'When I took my place on the ice with the others I was determined to die for Jesus. We sang hymns to keep our faith strong. Then, as the fierce cold ate into our bones, the singing died away. First one man, then another, sank to the ice. As they perished around me my courage waned. In the middle of the night, when all my comrades had dropped dead, I stumbled into the hut.'

'I don't understand this!' exclaimed the governor. 'There are twenty bodies out there. I counted —' He broke off suddenly. His gaze had fallen on one of the dead men. It was the army captain. He turned to the prisoner, his eyes round with shock. 'How did this happen?'

'He watched my friends fall one by one. You could see in his face how much he admired their bravery. Then when I – the last – gave up, he walked out and took my place. He died a Christian.'

Bit of a Giggle

The Irish have a saying: 'A woman told me that another woman said . . .' They use it when about to tell a story that has been passed from mouth to mouth, gaining new details with every telling, but which is probably untrue. The tale that follows is told in many English cities, often with names and places supplied. Clearly it cannot have happened in all these cities. Most likely it occurred in none. But it just might.

Gary and his two mates were strolling back from the chippy one evening, hands in pockets. They spoke little, for all three were profoundly bored. Life on a council estate on the outskirts of the city held little excitement for lively teenagers. There was nothing to do, they complained, often and bitterly. A few pubs and churches were the only meeting-places. Sixteen-year old Gary was too young for the pub and believed himself to be too old for the church.

As they walked past a telephone-box Gary said, 'I say, let's have a bit of a giggle.' The three boys, laughing and pushing each other, squeezed into the box. Gary picked up the phone and dialled the operator. A man's voice replied.

'Good evening, my good man,' said Gary in his best imitation of a posh accent. 'Would you be so good as to put me through to my good friend, the Queen? I seem to have lost her number.'

'Look, mate,' came the operator's weary voice, 'why don't you —'

Crash! Gary rammed the phone down on the rest. 'I'll bet that made his ears sing,' he laughed. He picked up the phone again and listened. 'Cor!' he exclaimed in disgust, 'I've wrecked it. Out of order. Let's get out of here.'

They continued their unhurried saunter along the wide pavement. Twilight was falling, and the street-lamps had begun to cast their gentle orange glow. Idly chatting, they passed the lighted windows of the Three Feathers and crossed the playing-fields. A hundred yards farther on Gary bade his friends goodnight and turned in at his garden gate. As soon as he entered the front door his mother rushed down the stairs. 'Gary, for God's sake,' she shouted. 'It's your father . . . some kind of seizure. Phone for the ambulance.'

The boy was off and running in a flash, his mind gripped by terror. His father had come home early from work that day with chest pains. Suddenly Gary remembered that he had broken the call-box phone. Cursing himself, he changed direction. He would have to use the one in the shopping centre, half a mile farther on. He sped along pencil-straight roads flanked by trim houses, reached the call-box, dialled 999 and gasped out his cry for help. Then, panting from his exertions, he made his way home.

The ambulance stood outside the house. The ambulance-man met him in the hall. 'I'm sorry, son,' he said, his eyes gentle with pity. 'We were just too late. If we'd been a few minutes earlier . . .'

Tact

'Dad, what is tact?' asked Clive, looking up from his book.

Mr White put down his newspaper. 'Tact is . . . let me see. Tact means not saying anything to hurt people's feelings. Or *doing* anything. Oh dear, I'm putting this badly. Tell you what, I know a story that shows what tact is.'

'Oh, good,' said Clive.

'A couple of hundred years ago there lived a one-eyed king. He was very touchy about his affliction. Anyone who mentioned it in his hearing – however innocently – lost the king's friendship on the spot. He was too proud to wear a patch, preferring to go about with one eyelid permanently closed. This made him look odd but no one dared to say so.

'Now, this king had a good friend who was an artist. They had known each other since their student days. Then the painter began to notice that the king was growing cold towards him. Long silences and silly rows told him that their friendship was in danger.

'One day the two men went stag-hunting. As they trudged along, rifles slung over their shoulders, the king said, "I want you to paint a portrait of me."

'"Certainly, your majesty," the artist answered, but his heart sank. He knew what the king was up to. A portrait would show the useless eye. The king would fly into a rage and break off their friendship. But, being a clever fellow, the painter thought he saw a way out of his problem. "I'll paint you in profile," he went on, "just as you are shown on our coins. The side view of your face looks really striking and I promise you that the picture will be first class." And, he added to himself, I shan't need to paint the injured eye.

'The king stopped. He directed at the artist a glare that seemed all the more piercing because it came from a single source. "You will paint me in full-face," he snapped. "You will show me exactly as I am."

'"Yes, your majesty," said the painter.

'For three months he worked alone in his studio, allowing no one to see his work. Then he sent a message to the king informing him that the portrait was finished. Next day his royal friend arrived with a group of noblemen. The nobles were agog with excitement, for they knew very well what was in the air. As they stood behind the king they watched with tense expressions as the artist removed the cloth that covered the painting.

'The picture showed the king full-length, in hunting garb, facing the viewer. His rifle was cradled in his shoulder as he took aim at an unseen stag. His good eye squinted along the barrel and the missing one, closed in the style of a marksman, looked quite natural.

'The king stared. The nobles waited. Then their royal master let out a peal of hearty laughter. He went to the artist, put his arms around him and said, "My dear old friend, I'll never fall out with anyone who takes such pains to spare my feelings."'

Mr White stopped. Clive smiled and said, 'And that's tact?'

'That's tact.'

The Resurrection Flower

Many charming stories have grown up around the birth of Jesus, but none more appealing than that of the resurrection plant. Its Latin name is *sempervivum*, which means 'ever-living'.

When Joseph was warned in a dream that Herod intended to kill Jesus he lost no time in preparing for the journey to Egypt. No doubt he had heard stories of Herod's cruelty. Caesar Augustus had remarked: 'I'd rather be Herod's pig than his son.' By this he referred to the fact that Herod had killed his own son but would never kill his pig, for eating its flesh was forbidden by Jewish law.

The little family set out on the long journey through bare and dangerous country. They picked their way along stony paths that hugged the mountain slopes. Mary, still weak from childbirth, rode on the donkey, the baby Jesus cradled in her protecting arms. Joseph walked ahead, leading the animal by the halter. They avoided well-trodden roads for fear of Herod's soldiers. By day the winter sun warmed them but the nights were cruelly cold.

One afternoon they stopped to rest in a rocky mountain pass. The sun shone from an empty sky, making stones and sand hot

to the touch. There was not another living creature to be seen in that harsh brown landscape. Mary sat against a rock, her baby in her lap. Then she spied a little withered plant. Its downy leaves, now dry and curled, formed a low rosette. Poor little thing, thought Mary, dead from lack of water. She reached down and gently touched the plant.

The change began at once. A rich green colour spread through the leaves. They rose and stretched like a child greeting a new day. From the centre of the rosette a slender stem emerged. It reached gratefully upwards before Mary's wondering gaze. At the top it put out tiny clusters of delicate pink flowers.

So men called it the resurrection plant. Resurrection means 'rising from the dead'. Some said that the flower returned to life to show that Jesus would one day do the same. Others read the lesson that goodness never wholly dies in men's hearts, but will revive and flower again at the touch of a single act of kindness.

The Miser's Bargain

Many years ago there lived a miser who never missed a chance to make a few pennies. One day he took a piece of cloth to the tailor who lived around the corner. 'Can you make me a cap from this material?' he asked.

'Certainly,' replied the tailor after a quick look at the cloth.

'How much?'

'Two shillings.'

The miser's face twisted with pain at the thought of spending so much money. 'That's far too dear. Have pity on a poor old man. Will you make two caps for that price?'

The tailor stared at him with distaste. 'All right.'

'God bless you, young man.' The miser's lips parted in a smile that revealed his yellow teeth. He went on: 'What about making four? It wouldn't be all that much trouble to a fine craftsman like you.'

'I'll make four,' agreed the tailor.

'For the same price?' asked the old man quickly.

'Yes.'

The miser's voice was husky with gratitude as he said, 'I'll remember you in my prayers. But look, you could just as easily make six. You would earn my life-long thanks if you gave me six.'

The tailor consented to make six. The old man, sure by now that he could make an even better bargain, pressed him to raise the number to eight. The tailor agreed. Then he asked for ten. The man behind the counter nodded. 'Ten it is,' he said.

The miser hurried off rubbing his hands together in joy at the splendid stroke of business he had done. Nothing gave him more pleasure than getting something for nothing. A week later he came back to collect his headgear. The tailor produced ten dinky little caps that would have fitted neatly on a child's doll. Flushing with rage the old man exclaimed: 'You don't really expect me to wear those!'

'I don't care whether you wear them or not so long as you pay me for them,' replied the other calmly. 'You asked me to make ten caps from a piece of cloth and I did so, using up all the material. Now you've got to pay. You stingy people must learn that your meanness sometimes leaves you worse off.'

Loudly the miser swore and blustered but the tailor stood firm. Finally the old man grudgingly handed over the money and left, a good deal wiser than when he had entered.

127

Lord and Ladybird

Everyone likes ladybirds. Gardeners are grateful to them for eating the tiny pests that attack their flowers. Children are attracted by their spotted domes and their sudden flight in a blur of concealed wings. French country folk call them 'God's little creatures'. They tell a stange old tale to explain the charming nickname.

There was once a lord whose lands stretched farther than a day's walk. He had a younger brother of whom he was very fond. One day this brother was found beaten to death in a field. The lord, beside himself with raging grief, ordered his servants to spare no effort to find the murderer. He swore the killer would die.

On the following day he was approached by Crondas, the steward who managed his estates. 'My lord, I have caught the murderer,' he announced with grim satisfaction.

'Are you sure? Are you quite sure?' The voice trembled with fury.

'Yes.'

'Fetch him,' snapped his master.

A young farm-worker was dragged in. In a voice shrill with despair he denied any part in the murder. Crondas took out a purse and a gold ring. 'I found these in this man's cottage,' he said.

'They were my brother's,' declared the lord. 'Young man, it is clear that you are guilty of a vile murder. You shall die tomorrow.'

The prisoner was taken away to spend his last night in a cell. Shortly afterwards a group of villagers came to plead for his life. They did not believe he was guilty, their spokesman said. The young man was hard-working, clever and gentle. Never had he been known to raise his hand to another person. 'He wouldn't hurt a fly,' the man finished. But the lord, a merciful man by nature, angrily sent them packing.

Next morning a silent crowd gathered to watch the execution. Crondas piled bundles of wood around the post at which the convicted man was to be burnt. His master sat nearby. The farm-worker was led in by armed soldiers. He begged to be allowed to say a last prayer for his soul. The lord nodded his consent. The prisoner bent his knee to kneel down. Then he noticed that he was about to crush a ladybird on the ground below him. Tenderly he picked up the insect between thumb and forefinger. The ladybird walked a little way along his finger, then took off and flew on to Crondas' hand. The steward squashed it with his other hand.

The young man finished his prayer. Soldiers tied him to the post. Crondas stepped forward with a burning torch.

'Stop!' The lord's voice rang out clear and strong. 'This man is innocent. At the point of death he could not bear to kill an insect. How then could he have killed a human being?'

'But my lord,' protested Crondas, 'the purse and the ring —'

'— were secretly hidden in his cottage to make him seem guilty.' His master's voice had risen to a shout. 'They were placed there by the man who murdered my brother. By the man who "discovered" them. By you, Crondas.'

The steward's face turned pale and his lips trembled. 'Yes, it's true. He found out that I was stealing from you and said he was going to tell you. I killed him to protect myself.'

The farm-worker was set free and Crondas was put to death in his place. As for the ladybird, everyone was sure that God had sent it to save the young man's life. Ever since then the French have had a warm regard for the little fellow.

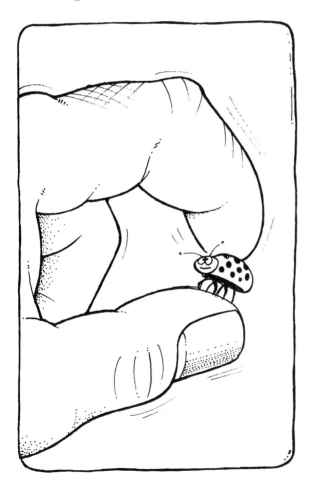

Old Bert's Blankets

Old Bert lived alone in a terraced house in Birmingham. The Second World War was at its height. Many a night the city's air-raid sirens sounded their strange and fearful cry. With weary patience people prepared for the attack of enemy bombers. Bert, like many others, used to go out to an air-raid shelter in his back garden. It was small but strong, with solid brick sides and a round, corrugated-iron roof. Here he would lie on a camp bed and read until the raid was over or, if it lasted long enough, tuck himself up snugly and sleep until morning.

One night as he lay in his shelter and listened to the boom of guns and bombs the old man felt very sad. How he wished he were young again, so that he could go out and fight to help bring this terrible war to an end. Or if he were only a few years younger he could become an air-raid warden and assist those who had been bombed out of their houses. But here he was, a feeble old man, sitting around waiting to die, unable to do a thing for any of the younger folk. He thought, 'If only I'd been able to give the vicar something for his church hall. It was splendid of him to turn it into a sleeping-place for bombed-out families. But I'm so poor that I couldn't think of a thing to give him. I've no extra food. The only bedclothes I've got are my wedding present blankets and I wouldn't give those to *anybody*.'

Bert smiled as he thought of the two green blankets folded in a soft pile in his wardrobe. They had been a present from Elsie's – his wife's – mother. Elsie had always been proud of them because they looked so expensive. How angry she had been when he fell asleep with a lighted cigarette in his hand! She had mended them so cleverly that you would hardly notice the square woollen patches, but from that day forward she had kept them to be used only when a special visitor came. Bert spoke aloud: 'I couldn't give Elsie's best blankets away.'

Next morning he called at the vicarage and handed in the blankets. 'Are you sure you can spare them?' asked the vicar. 'These are fine things.'

'I'm sure,' said the old man with a shrug of his shoulders. 'They're only gathering dust in my wardrobe.' He hurried off before he could change his mind, for he was not certain whether he felt glad or sorry.

A week later Bert was pouring himself a second cup of tea when the sirens wailed. 'Here we go again,' he groaned aloud. Like many people who live alone he often talked to himself. 'Am I going to rush out to the back or shall I wait and have my cuppa?' He decided to finish it before going to the shelter, but he never did. A mighty bang filled his ears and a huge weight struck the back of his head. Everything went black.

Old Bert woke up in bed with the vicar bending over him. 'How's my house?' he murmured faintly.

The vicar looked uncomfortable. 'Ruined, I'm afraid. But you mustn't worry. The doctor says you'll be fine. Are you warm enough?'

'Sure,' replied Bert, tucking his hands under the coverlet and feeling the blankets. Suddenly a strange expression stole over his face. Then his eyes lit up in a delighted smile. His fingers had found, in the corner of the blanket, a square woollen patch.

Swindled

A rich merchant went to a builder and said, 'You've done a lot of good work for me in the past. My finest store-rooms and mills were constructed by you. Now I want you to build me a house. Oh, it's not for me, but for someone I prize very highly. Make it the best building you've ever raised. Use only the most skilled craftsmen and the strongest materials. Don't worry about the cost. I'll pay whatever you ask.'

'I'll take the job,' said the builder, 'and I assure you I'll do my very best . . .' He waited until his client had left the office before he added: '. . . to swindle you out of every penny I can.' He needed money desperately. Gambling and wild spending had left him neck-deep in debt. Now the merchant had given him his chance.

He started work on the new house, using the cheapest materials he could scrape together. Mouldy cement, second-hand pipes, third-rate nails, wood salvaged from derelict houses – he patched them all up into something resembling a house. Craftily he exerted all his skill to make the outside as attractive as possible. Inside, he concealed his shoddy workmanship with equal cunning. When the job was finished he gazed at the building and said, 'It looks fine now but in a couple of years it will be falling to pieces. But by that time I'll be out of debt.'

Next day the merchant came to see the completed house. His face lit up with satisfaction. 'You've done wonders,' he said simply.

'I certainly have,' replied the builder, laughing inwardly. He produced the key and tendered it to his client. The merchant refused it with a shake of his hand, his kind little eyes twinkling. 'It's yours,' he said.

'Mine? But, but . . .' stuttered the builder.

'My friend, you worked so well for me in the past that I decided to reward you. This house is yours. You deserve it.'

The builder managed a sickly smile. 'Great heavens,' he thought, 'I'm going to have to live in this ramshackle booby-trap. Yes, I really deserve it.'

The Inchcape Rock

In the old days many a tall-masted sailing ship foundered on the Inchcape Rock. It is a jagged reef nearly half a mile long that lies off the coast of Scotland in the grey North Sea. Uncounted sailors died there when their ships ran aground by accident or were hurled on to the rocks in one of the storms for which that sea is feared.

The Abott of Aberbrothock made up his mind to halt the tragic loss of lives. He and his monks placed a bell on the rock. It hung from a short wooden gallows. When high seas washed over the reef they set the bell ringing. Its deep tones boomed a warning far out to sea, alerting ships to danger. The number of wrecks fell sharply. Sailors everywhere blessed the life-saving work of the good monk.

One day a pirate named Ralph the Rover sailed up to the Bell Rock, as it was now called. With a party of his rascals he rowed ashore and cut the rope that supported the bell. Down it crashed on the steep crag. Then the bell rolled towards the sea, booming from rock to rock in its swift fall. As it slid beneath the waves its iron tongue gave a final clang and was lost forever. Laughing at his own wickedness, Ralph the Rover rowed back to his ship.

Next day he set sail for the Spanish Main. There he lay in wait for the tall galleons heading for Spain, laden with the wealth of the Americas. He plundered ship after ship, gathering enough treasure to make him rich for the rest of his life. Then he pointed his ship towards his native Scotland.

As he drew near land a sudden storm arose. The wind shrieked fiercely and the sea became a range of onrushing watery hills. Rain fell in a dense curtain, blotting out all sight of land. Ralph's ship breasted the mighty waves in a desperate dash for home. All at once there was a great tearing noise, and the wooden craft crashed on the Bell Rock. Not a single sailor survived. Storytellers of that time claimed that the last sound Ralph the Rover heard as he sank beneath the waves was the ghostly clangour of the lost bell, tolling for his death.

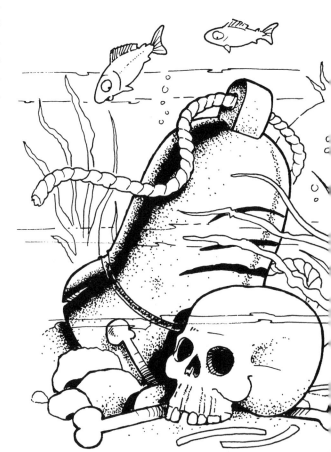

The Thief and the Monk

(Adapted from the *Apophthegmata Patrum*, by Anan Isho)

Far out in the desert a band of monks lived in a great stone house. They spent their lives praying, studying their sacred books and sheltering the poor. One of their number – whose name has not come down to us – was an old man who was much loved for his gentle and forgiving nature. All he owned was a bible. It had cost him eighteen darics and he valued it more highly than anything else in the world. He kept it in a hole in the wall of his cell.

A stranger once came to stay with the monks. They treated him with their usual kindness. He visited the old man in his cell and saw the bible. The precious book, hand-written and bound in soft leather, filled him with greed. Craftily he watched the monk hide it in the hole. A short while later the stranger stole the bible when its owner was out and fled towards the nearest village. When the old monk discovered his loss he knew at once who the thief was. His brother monks urged him to set out after the stranger but mildly he refused.

Meanwhile the thief, eager to sell the bible before the monk caught up with him, went to the village market. 'It's yours for sixteen darics,' he told the would-be buyer.

'That's a stiff price,' replied the man. 'Let me take it to a friend of mine who knows about these things. If he agrees with your price I'll pay it.'

The thief consented and the buyer left. He returned the next day saying, 'Yes, my friend says the book is worth sixteen darics.' He took out his purse.

'Who is your friend?' asked the thief.

To his amazement the buyer gave the name of the old monk. 'What . . . what did he say?' asked the thief.

'Oh, he examined it with care and turned the pages over lovingly – almost as if it was his own book. Then he told me the price was fair and I should buy it.' He held out a handful of coins.

Suddenly the thief was overcome with shame. The good old man had not followed him. Nor had he given him away to the buyer. Indeed, he was willing to see his dearest possession sold in the market by the man who had stolen it. The thief came to a decision. 'I've changed my mind,' he told the surprised buyer. 'I'm not going to sell the bible.'

He hurried to the monk and begged his forgiveness. It was gladly given. When he tried to hand over the bible the old man refused to take it. The thief should keep it and learn from it, he insisted. Finally, after some argument, he took the book back. The thief joined the band of monks and spent the rest of his life in prayer and good works.

A Tale of Two Dogs

How sweet life would be if every true-life story ended as it does in fairy tales. There the good guys overcome their troubles and live happily ever after while the baddies come to a nasty end. In the real world it is often the other way round. Here are two dog stories that make the point clear.

When Martin moved into the new house he had worked so hard to buy he took his dog Fred with him. After all, his mother told him, a young man living on his own in a big house needs company. Martin was delighted to take the hairy mongrel, which he had owned since it was a pup. They settled down in their new home. Soon Martin felt as if he had lived there all his life and Fred, to judge from his contented behaviour, was equally at his ease.

One August day Martin locked his front door, bundled Fred into the back seat of his car and set off for a caravan holiday in Cornwall. As soon as he had unpacked he took the dog for a walk in the woods. Joyously Fred bounded among the trees, sniffing the strange scents of the country-side. Within a few minutes he was nowhere to be seen. Martin became anxious. He shouted the dog's name. Nothing happened. He shouted again and again. There was no response. He tramped the woods until darkness fell but Fred· was lost.

Next day he went to the police station. They could not help him. He dropped in to the newspaper office and arranged to have an advertisement inserted. The rest of the day he spent searching the beach and woods, but with no success.

The next two weeks proved to be the most miserable holiday Martin had ever spent. Every morning he rose hopefully and every night he went to bed disappointed. He was almost glad when the day arrived for him to go home. Gloomily he got into his car, cast a last look at the woods where Fred had vanished and set off for the city. When he stopped outside his front door you'll never guess what he found sitting on the doorstep. Yes, you're perfectly right – fourteen bottles of milk. He had forgotten to tell the milkman he was going away!

If you think *that* is a rotten story you cannot have heard the one about Hans, the stray dog. He turned up one day in a village high in the Alps, dirty and starving. First, he attacked every cat in sight. Next he knocked over two dustbins, spilling their contents in the snow, and hungrily scoffed the scraps of food. The villagers chased him out. He came back, slinking around the back doors, stealing any bits of food he could lay his paws on, frightening old ladies and making an all-round pest of himself.

One night the mayor and the policeman stood in the square looking up at the mountain. 'I'm really worried this time,' said the mayor. 'Just look at that north ridge.' He pointed to the huge spur of rock that hung over the village.

'I've never seen so much snow on it,'

said the policeman, his face creased in a troubled frown. 'If we should have an avalanche now . . .' He did not finish the sentence, but the mayor knew what he meant. A hundred years before, when the north ridge had been piled high with snow in just the same fashion, a massive avalanche had swept over the village, killing thirty-two people.

At that moment Hans dashed past the two men, a chunk of raw steak clamped between his jaws. From around the corner came the angry yell of a furious housewife. 'I'm going to kill that dog tomorrow,' declared the policeman.

'We've got to get rid of him,' agreed the mayor.

'First thing tomorrow morning I'll get out the old shotgun and finish him off,' said the policeman.

As darkness fell that night Hans curled up to sleep against the bakery wall. In the middle of the night a sound woke him. He started up, ears pricked. The noise was deep and rumbling, and growing louder by the second. He looked up. High on the mountainside a broad tide of snow was sweeping down, swelling as it rushed on, heading straight for the sleeping village.

Hans was the only living creature aware of the danger – the only one who could warn the humans of their peril. Without a sound he loped swiftly down the road to the safety of the lowlands, while the mighty avalanche crashed on the roof-tops, killing everyone.

The Vanishing Bear

The owner of The Bear, a country pub, was a simple but crafty fellow. He once went to an artist and said, 'I'd like you to paint an inn-sign to hang outside my pub. But first, how much would you charge?'

'Fifteen pounds,' replied the painter.

'*Fifteen pounds*!' echoed the publican, wrinkling his face in a well-acted display of shock. 'That's far too much. I know another painter who will do it for ten.' He thought, 'Of course there is no other painter but I hope to beat down your price.'

'Really?' said the artist. He thought, 'I'm sure there is no other painter. You're just trying to bluff me out of five pounds.' Aloud he asked, 'What kind of picture did you want?'

'A bear, a grizzly bear.'

The artist scratched his chin. 'Chained or unchained?'

'Unchained.'

'I'll do it for ten pounds.'

A week later the publican called to collect the sign. He liked the vivid painting of an upright grizzly, its mouth gaping in a lop-sided snarl. After paying the artist he hurried home and hung the sign above the pub door. Soon it was the talk of the countryside. People walked miles just to see it. Every night the pub was full, and so was the publican's till.

A short time afterwards a fierce storm raged during the hours of darkness. All

night long thunder crackled and rain drummed on the windows. Next morning the publican went out to see if there was any damage. When he looked up at the sign his mouth fell open in dismay. The bear had vanished! The square of wood was totally blank.

He dashed off to the painter's house and broke the bad news. The painter took it calmly. 'I'm not a bit surprised,' he remarked. 'It was such a terrible night that the bear must have run off to find shelter in the caves.'

'Ah, I see,' said the publican, his foolish face lighting up in understanding.

'Now if he had been *chained* he couldn't have run away,' said the artist.

'Yes, what a pity.'

'Tell you what, I'll paint you a chained bear.'

'Oh yes, please.'

'For *fifteen* pounds.'

'Well, all right.'

So a new bear wearing a strong chain took his place outside the pub. He never ran away, however bad the weather. Nor did the publican ever try to drive a crooked bargain again, having found that honest dealing is best. The artist never told him that he had painted the first bear in water-colours, which wash away in the rain, and the second in oils, which do not.

St Nicholas

Long, long ago there lived a rich man and his wife who had no children. As time passed this became a great sorrow to them. They longed for a son more than anything else in the world. 'Let's pray to St Nicholas,' said the wife.

'Who's he?' asked her husband.

'No one is very sure. Some say he was a bishop. Lots of people pray to him and swear he can perform miracles.'

So the couple began to pray to the saint. The man promised that if a son was born to him he would journey to the saint's tomb and place a precious drinking-vessel on it. To their delight the wife gave birth to a boy. The rich man told a craftsman to make a golden goblet of the finest design. When it arrived the man was so dazzled by its beauty that he decided to keep it for himself. The saint, he thought, would have to be content with something a little less superb. He ordered the goldsmith to make another goblet, one that was not so expensive.

A few years later the rich man set sail for the saint's burial-place, taking with him his son and the two drinking-cups. He handed the fine goblet to his little boy and asked him to fill it with sea-water. The lad bent over the side and fell into the sea, vanishing without trace. The heartbroken father continued his journey and finally reached the tomb of St Nicholas. He took the second-rate goblet and tried to place it on the marble surface. To his astonishment an unseen force pushed it away. He tried again and again but the invisible barrier prevented him from setting down the cup.

Suddenly his little son stood before him, pink and healthy, clutching the first goblet. St Nicholas had saved him from drowning, he explained. The rich man took both goblets and reverently placed them on the marble tomb.

Stories like this one were woven around the name of the saint but we know very little about his life. It is probable that he was born at the Turkish port of Patara. He certainly became Bishop of Myra. Tales of his kindness and of his unearthly powers passed down through the centuries, losing nothing in the telling. Many of the stories claim that he could send his body in an instant to a distant place, like space-travellers on television. In time people came to believe that he had a special love for children. He gave them presents on his feast day, 6 December, they said. Artists began to paint him as a laughing, red-cheeked old fellow, draped in furs against the winter weather, carrying a sack of gifts for children. There are no prizes for guessing what we call St Nicholas nowadays.

Captain Beynon's Parrot

When old Captain Beynon announced that he would soon go to live with his daughter in Cardiff everyone wondered if he would take his parrot with him. The handsome red and blue bird was the smartest talking bird in Wales, if not the whole wide world. He had only to hear a thing once, folk said, and he could repeat it word for word.

The day after the sea-captain made his announcement David, Glyn and Linda came to visit him. They were neighbours' children. All had been born and lived their short lives in the tiny fishing-port. They often called in on their way home from school to spend an hour chatting to the old man and his parrot. 'Well, are you going to take Barney with you?' asked Linda boldly.

Captain Beynon grinned and stroked his grey beard. 'No,' he said, 'I reckon I'm too old to look after him properly. I'm going to give him to one of you three kids.'

The children's eyes widened in surprise and hope. David was the first to find his voice. 'Which of us?'

'That depends,' replied the captain. 'Tell you what I'll do. I'll let each of you in

turn take Barney home to live with you for a week. Now it's not all fun taking care of a bird. There are plenty of boring little chores to be done. You'll have to feed him and water him and look after him. It'll give you a chance to make up your mind whether you really want to keep him.'

'Oh, I do,' said the children with one voice.

The old man's face crinkled in a strange little smile. 'We'll see. When you've all had a turn at looking after him I'll make up my mind which one of you I'll give him to. Now you're the oldest, Glyn, so you may have him first. Take him with you now and bring him back this day next week.'

Glyn took the parrot and the children left. A week later the boy returned the bird and Linda took it home. Then came David's turn. When he brought Barney back to the captain's house the old man thanked him and said he would let them know his decision very soon.

Two days later Captain Beynon sent for the children. They sat on the edge of their chairs, tense, eyes fixed on the ancient sailor. 'I suppose you all want to keep him,' he said.

'Yes.'

'Definitely.'

'Yes.'

The captain nodded. 'I thought so. Well, kids, I haven't been completely honest with you. Remember I said that you could keep Barney for a week to see if you really wanted him? What I really wished to know was how each of you behaves in your own home – whether you would give my bird the loving attention he needs. And I've just found out.'

'But, but how?' stammered Glyn.

'Easy. When Barney came back from his week with you, Glyn, he kept saying, "I can't be bothered. I have no time." After his return from Linda's home he repeated: "Ask somebody else. You always pick on me. Why me? I'm too tired." So I knew that you two are the sort of children who won't help with the chores around the house – the sort who couldn't be trusted to look after my parrot day after day. But when Barney came back from David he kept repeating: "Need any help? Can I give you a hand?" Then I knew I'd found the kind of busy, reliable person to care for my bird.'

Smiling, David rose to take the parrot.

Happily Ever After?

Never try to re-live the pleasures of your past; no delight is ever quite as sharp the second time around. So our wise men tell us, and they should know. Happiness is a fragile blend of persons, places and events that can never be put together again. To attempt it is to destroy tender memories. If you argue against this gloomy view they may tell you the tale of Wan Sung.

He learned to play chess soon after he began to walk. Chess is a game which some very young children can play with dazzling cleverness. Wan Sung swiftly showed that he was one. His family were astonished at the speed with which he picked up the moves. They watched with pride as the infant, kneeling on a chair, skilfully moved the carved pieces on their black and white squares. Within a year he could beat any player in his Chinese town. By the time he was twelve he had defeated every great player in the land except one – the champion of China. A game between them was arranged. It was contested on the stage of a large hall and was watched by packed rows of silent but excited experts.

The game lasted nearly two hours. The onlookers followed its progress, move by move, on giant boards set up at the back of the stage. Neither player showed the least emotion as their tiny armies clashed. Behind the blank faces, however, their

minds throbbed in a thrilling mixture of hope and fear.

At first one player seemed to be winning, then the other. Pawns, the humble foot-soldiers in each army, plodded towards the enemy. Crafty bishops attacked slantwise. Knights launched nasty surprises with their offbeat sideways

leaps. Powerful queens and rooks raged around the board. Finally the champion turned over his king in a gesture of surrender. A storm of applause flowed over the delighted Wan Sung. He felt he could burst with happiness.

All of a sudden a goblin appeared beside him. 'Well done, lad,' he said, showing his pointed teeth in a twisted smile. 'I'm so pleased that I'll use my magic skills to grant you any wish. What do you long for more than anything in the world?'

The wonder-boy needed no time to think. 'Just let me live the last two hours all over again,' he begged.

At once the hands of the clock ran back. Wan Sung found himself sitting down to start the game. He tasted again the tension, the growing belief that he could win, the final attack on the champion's king and the thrill of joy when he gained the victory. Then the goblin appeared, granted Wan Sung his wish and the game began again. You see, that was the last of the events of the two hours the boy had asked for. When the second game ended the goblin appeared . . .

But this story has no end. As soon as Wan Sung rose from the table he sat down again for a replay. At this very moment he may be playing that game for the millionth time. He will go on repeating it forever. You may be sure that his delight in winning has by now changed into the bitterest of sorrows.

The Sting

The number of stories about Nasrudin must run into hundreds. They describe his amazing career as a swindler, priest, village headman, practical joker and smuggler. All these tales bring out the man's cunning mind and impish sense of humour.

One of the best tales tells of the time Nasrudin found himself poor and jobless. He had one tiny pot in which to cook his food. Now the man next door owned a big copper pot which Nasrudin envied greatly. He decided that he must possess it, by fair means or foul. One day he knocked at his neighbour's door and asked if he might borrow the big pot for a few days. The neighbour, a rather stupid man, gladly agreed and Nasrudin took it home.

Next day he returned the utensil. In it he had placed his own little pot. The neighbour stared. 'What's this?' he demanded.

Nasrudin's face lit up in a sugary smile. 'Your pot has given birth to a little one. Isn't it wonderful? Isn't he sweeeeeeet?' The rascal tickled the small pot with his index finger, cooing, 'Who's a naughty boy, then?'

The neighbour goggled at Nasrudin. This man must be crackers, he thought. He thinks that pots can have babies. Aloud he said, 'Ah yes, I knew she was about to give birth. Thank you, I'll take good care of mother and baby.' He took the pots into his house, chuckling at his own cleverness.

Some time later Nasrudin borrowed the big pot again. Next morning he called in at his neighbour's. His face bore a look of deep sadness. 'I have tragic news for you, my friend,' he said. 'Your pot died last night.'

The other man burst out laughing. 'You're crazy,' he chortled. 'Pots can't die. Everyone knows that.'

'Oh yes they can,' insisted Nasrudin. 'Remember, your pot gave birth, and everything that can give birth can die – indeed, *must* die. You'll be glad to know that I buried her reverently in the big field – I'm not sure where, for it was dark.'

The neighbour was dumb-struck. Having agreed that lifeless objects could give birth he was forced to accept that they could die. By trying to swindle the apparently simple-minded Nasrudin he himself had been robbed. Furious with himself, and determined never to try to cheat anyone again, he slammed the door in the trickster's face. Nasrudin went merrily back to his home where the big pot, full of a tasty soup, simmered on the fire.

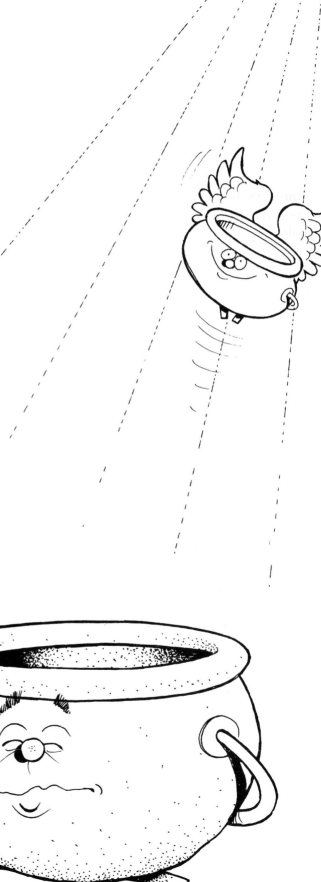

Five Fingers

Take a look at your right hand, palm upwards. On the left is Mr Little Finger, the smallest of the five. Americans call him the pinkie. He is not very strong and it is hard to think of any job he can perform on his own. In times gone by certain well-bred persons, while holding a teacup, used to stretch out their little finger. They believed this to be a mark of good manners.

Next to him stands Mr Feeble Finger, so called because he is very weak. Indeed, he can hardly move without the help of some of his brothers. Try waggling him back and forth and you will see what I mean.

Then comes Mr Middle Finger. He is the tallest of the lot but I am afraid he is no more useful than the other two.

Mr Pointing Finger stands beside him. He is the most active of all. In addition to pointing he presses doorbells, helps pick up small objects and, when wagged in the air, adds force to what we say when we scold children or make a public speech. There is no doubt that Mr Pointing Finger is the most skilful of the brothers.

Last of all is Mr Chubby. Short and broad, he is the strongest of the five brothers. He can push harder – he is very good with drawing pins – and we sometimes raise him upright above our clenched fist to mean 'everything is fine'.

Now each of these little fellows cannot do very much by himself. But when he works closely with his brothers he can perform wonders. He can paint a marvellous picture, play music to delight the ear, heal a wounded body, catch a flying ball or control a speeding horse. He can also do such ordinary but important jobs as tying laces, darning socks and using a knife and fork.

People are like fingers. Most of them cannot achieve very much on their own but when they work together there is no limit to what they can do.

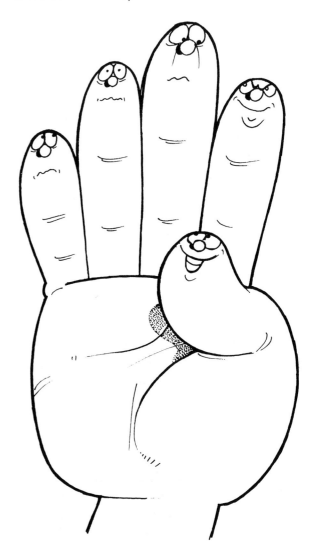

Anselm's Dream

The farmer and his seven sons stood before the giant stone. Although its base was sunk in the ground it towered over them. The monks were ranged in a semi-circle on the hilltop, their eyes fixed hopefully on the farmer and his boys. At a signal from the father all eight leaned against the stone and pushed with all their force. They grunted with the effort, and sweat dampened their flushed faces. At first there was no movement. Then the great pile shuddered and shifted. With an almighty thump it toppled backwards, rolled down the hillside and crashed into the sea.

Anselm woke from his dream. In a state of high excitement he dressed and rushed out of the monastery. He hurried to the farmer's cottage and told him: 'I want you to help me. You know of course that we monks are building a new monastery on the top of the hill. Well, we've cleared away all the stones except one. It's a huge brute that we simply can't shift.

'Now last night I dreamt that you and your seven sons came and pushed it down the hillside. That dream was a message from God. He often guides my in my sleep. Will you and your boys make my dream come true?'

The farmer consented to do all he could to help. Next morning he climbed to the hilltop with his sons. Anselm stood with his brother monks and watched them roll up their sleeves. They leaned against the lofty stone and pushed. Nothing happened. They heaved and shoved until sweat ran down their faces. The stone did not so much as quiver.

Anselm was amazed. Something is wrong here, he thought. Swiftly he counted the straining bodies. 'Look here,' he said to the farmer, 'you've brought only six sons. My dream said seven.'

'I didn't bring my youngest,' came the reply. 'He's only a little lad. He's not very strong.'

'Bring him tomorrow,' ordered Anselm.

Next day the little boy rolled up his sleeves beside his father and brothers. They pushed. Sweat dampened their flushed faces. At first there was no movement. Then the great pile shuddered and shifted. With an almighty thump it toppled backwards, rolled down the hillside and crashed into the sea.

Anselm told the monks: 'The youngest boy's feeble arms did the trick. Remember, when you take on a great task it is always the last little effort that brings success.'

Tongue

The story of Orula was being told in the West Indies long before Columbus landed there five hundred years ago. The copper-skinned islanders believed that there were many gods, the chief of whom was Obatala. He ruled the whole of space, his power reaching out to the farthest star. Naturally his duties kept him very busy.

One day he made up his mind to appoint a governor to the planet Earth – some young god who could rule wisely and take the burden off his shoulders. He gave the matter serious thought. Before reaching a decision he weighed up the talents of each of his heavenly brothers. His first choice was Orula, a young god who was much praised for his sharp common sense. But Obatala had doubts. Perhaps Orula was too young. Governing Earth was a hard task, for its people were known to be the most difficult creatures in the vast reaches of space. Obatala decided to give Orula a test. He said to the young god, 'Please prepare a meal for me, the most delicious dish you can cook.'

'As you wish, Lord of the Universe,' replied Orula, showing no trace of surprise. He left and returned some hours later, carrying a large round plate on which rested the meal he had cooked. It consisted of a portion of beef tongue hedged round with delicate little savouries. Obatala tasted some of the food, then declared: 'It is excellent. Now tell me, why did you choose tongue?'

'The tongue is a wonderful instrument for doing good,' said Orula. 'It can speak words of love and kindness, tell jokes, urge men to live nobly and comfort those in pain.'

The chief god said, 'That's a wise answer. Now go and cook the *worst* meal you can.' Orula bowed and left for the heavenly kitchens. When he had prepared the meal he set it before Obatala. The old god stared in surprise. On the plate lay a large portion of tongue. He picked it up and bit off a tiny piece. After chewing it for a few seconds he spat it out, his face wrinkling up with distaste. 'It's vile,' he announced. 'Why did you choose tongue a second time?'

'To show that the tongue can be a tool of evil as well as good. It can spread lies, inflict pain by means of cruel words and even persuade people to acts of wickedness.'

Obatala told him: 'Your words and actions have proved to me that you are a clear-headed young god. I hereby appoint you to rule the Earth, for everyone there is the mixture of good and evil you described in the tongue.'

A Stubborn Couple

Wise men through the ages have told us that if we believe we are in the right we must stand firm. Our history books praise noble men and women who suffered for their unchanging refusal to bend their will to others. We rightly admire the person who sticks to his beliefs, come hell or high water. However, this is all very well when a point of high principle is at stake but it can be carried too far in the hurly-burly of everyday life. Take the case of Farmer Brown and his missus.

The farmer arrived home – a one-room hut – after a tiring day in the fields. He was cold, hungry and as bad-tempered as a bag of cats. 'Is me tea ready?' he growled.

His wife, who had had a hard day in the house, gave him an angry look and slammed the pot down on the table. Suddenly the door was blown open by the bitter wind. Snowflakes danced in on the chilling rush of air.

'Shut the door,' snapped Mrs Brown.

'Shut it yourself,' her husband retorted.

'You shut it. You're nearest.'

'I'm exhausted,' said the farmer, sitting down heavily at the table. 'You've been lying around here all day. You shut it.'

'Definitely not.'

Farmer Brown glared. 'I'll tell you what, the first of us to speak must close the door.'

'Agreed.'

For the rest of the evening the only sound in the room was the crackle of logs on the fire. Not a word was spoken. The door lay open and the freezing wind blew freely around the hut. When bedtime came they undressed in silence, blue with cold, teeth chattering, and settled down in the big bed in the corner.

In the middle of the night a wild dog wandered into the hut. The unhappy pair were too frozen to get out of bed and chase it out. Each was too stubborn to break the silence by shouting at the animal. Helplessly they watched as the dog sprang up on to the dresser and scoffed all their bread and meat.

Next morning, after a shivering and sleepless night, they rose. Mrs Brown took her basket and set off for the village shop,

taking care to leave the door open behind her. The farmer waited indoors, as the barber was due that morning to trim his beard and moustache. Soon the barber arrived and said cheerfully, 'Good morning. How are you?'

Farmer Brown did not reply.

'I said "Good morning",' said the barber.

Silence.

He took out his scissors, soap and razor. He began his work, trying several times to start a conversation. His customer's lips remained firmly shut. At last, annoyed by the farmer's silence, he shaved the beard and moustache from one side of his face. Then he rubbed soot all over the obstinate fellow's forehead and ears.

At that moment Mrs Brown returned. At the sight of her husband's face, half bearded, half bald, she burst out laughing. 'You should see yourself!' she chuckled.

'You spoke!' cried the farmer, pointing a triumphant finger at her. Still laughing, she closed the door and handed him a mirror. He looked at himself and then he too broke into loud laughter.

Why the Robin's Breast is Red

'Brother braves,' said the Red Indian chief, 'I have asked you to my wigwam today to put a plan before you. You all know how we suffer when the Sun-god grows weak in winter. Cold winds pierce our tents and seem to settle in our very bones. What we need is fire. Now the only fire in our land burns in the wigwam of the three witches. They guard it jealously and will not permit anyone to take away a burning branch. We must steal this fire.'

'How?' asked a young brave.

'How,' answered the chief, raising his hand in greeting. Then, realizing his mistake, he said, 'Oh, you mean "How?"' Well, we shall need the help of our friends, the animals. They will play a vital part in the plan which I shall now unfold.'

The chief spoke for five minutes. The braves listened, nodding in agreement from time to time, then left, well satisfied. Next morning the three witches were crouching over their fire when the flap of their wigwam was lifted and the wolf entered. 'Let me warm myself at your fire,' he begged. 'I'm frozen.'

'All right,' growled the oldest of the long-nosed hags.

The wolf sat down at the fire. Then he threw back his head and gave a thunder-

ous sneeze. It was a signal. From outside the tent came a wild Indian war-cry. The witches rushed out to attack the enemy. The wolf seized a burning branch in his mouth. He dashed outside and tossed it to the deer. The deer sped off. Swiftly the witches mounted their broomsticks and zoomed after him. Just as they closed in the deer threw the burning stick to the robin. The robin, who in those distant days was a plain brown bird, caught the branch in his beak. He flew off, followed by the witches. Soon the fire had burned a red patch on his chest. He hastily dropped the flaming stick to the squirrel, who in turn passed it to the frog, who finally gave it to an Indian brave. The plan had worked. The Indians now had fire and the robin had a red breast.

But there is another account of how the robin earned his crimson front. Many years ago the cheeky little bird was flying over Jerusalem Looking down, he noticed a large crowd on a hilltop outside the city. They were clustered around three crosses on which hung dying men. One wore a crown of thorns. Tiny rivers of blood ran down his sweating face.

The robin's heart was moved to pity. Swooping down, he paused in flight in front of the dying man. He flapped his wings backwards and forwards, using them like fans, to cool the man's burning face. But he ventured too close and touched the bleeding forehead. His feathers were stained red. Every robin since then has worn that badge of honour. It is, we are told, a mark of gratitude from Jesus to the little bird that comforted his last hours.

A Dream of Power

Wu Pang worked from dawn to dusk in the rice-fields of old China. Being clever and energetic he was sickened by the thought of spending his life as a lowly farm-worker. One day he entered a country inn, ordered a bowl of bamboo soup and sat down in a corner. He felt deeply sorry for himself. An old priest, seeing the young man's miserable expression, asked, 'What's the matter, son?'

Wu Pang told him of his wretched life in the fields. 'I want to be somebody important,' he added. 'I long for power and riches. I dream of a high position, perhaps by the side of our great emperor, helping him to rule his vast lands.'

The old man looked at him with eyes full of concern. 'You look tired,' he said. 'Why don't you lie down for a few minutes while the landlord prepares your soup? Here, I'll lend you my own pillow.' He opened his travelling-bag and took out a pillow made of porcelain. It was hollow, and both surfaces bore strange painted signs.

Wu lay down in the corner, placed his head on the pillow and closed his eyes. At once the pillow seemed to swell. Wu jumped in alarm. Sure enough, the pillow was growing all the time. Now it was tall enough for him to step inside. He did so and walked to the other end. Imagine his shock when he found himself back in his rice-field.

All that winter Wu studied hard in the evenings. In the spring he passed his examinations with high marks and entered the civil service. Soon he was moved to a higher post. Swiftly he climbed the ladder of power, spurred on by his burning desire to reach the heights. He married the daughter of a rich merchant and bought a grand estate. Next he was appointed to the ruling council of ministers. Then came the greatest prize: the emperor made him his prime minister. His wildest dreams had come true.

Then his troubles began. Enemies, jealous of his power, plotted to bring him down. They spread foul lies about him.

The crowds which had lined the streets to cheer him now watched him pass in silent hatred. By underhand means the plotters managed to turn the emperor against him. He was arrested, tried and sentenced to death. On a cold morning he laid his head on the block and watched, terrified, as the executioner ran his thumb along the curved blade of his axe. The dreaded weapon rose and . . .

Wu Pang woke up, sweating and trembling. The old priest was smiling at him and the landlord was placing his bowl of soup on the table. The pillow lay under his head. It had all been a dream. 'You have taught me a lesson,' said the young man. 'Now I know that those who climb highest have farthest to fall.'

The Captive King

War broke out between two kings. Each gathered an army and marched into battle. The result was a resounding victory for one of them. He took the other king prisoner. He ordered his guards to throw the man into a deep, dried-up well from which he had no chance to escape. There he lived miserably, kept alive only by scraps of food thrown down by the guards.

One night as he lay shivering he heard a faint noise at the top of the well. He looked up. A man's head showed up against the night sky. 'Hush!' whispered the stranger. 'I'm going to get you out of here.' A thick rope slithered down to the king. 'Grab it,' came the voice. 'I'll pull at this end.'

Eagerly the king grasped the rope and began to haul himself up, planting his feet on the sides of the well. After a little while the stranger said, 'I'll bet you're thankful that I came along to rescue you.'

'Of course,' replied the king.

When the captive was halfway up the man said, 'No one else would take the risk I'm taking. You must be full of gratitude for what I'm doing.'

'Yes, yes,' gasped the king. 'But get on with it.'

At last the royal prisoner reached the top and lay panting in the darkness beside his rescuer. The man continued: 'I'm sure you'll never forget the bravery of a stranger who risked his own freedom to restore yours.'

The king gave him a long look which displayed no hint of gratitude. Then he raised his head and shouted: 'Guards, come quickly. The king is escaping. Come here. At the double!' All at once the darkness was filled with the clatter of running feet. In a few seconds the two men were surrounded by soldiers.

The stranger stared open-mouthed at the king. 'Why in heaven's name did you do that?'

'Because I'm already sick of hearing you remind me of how much I owe you. Because if I had escaped, my life would have been made a burden. You would have recalled my debt to you so often that I think I should have died. I prefer to be a prisoner. When you do a good deed don't keep bragging about it. By doing so you take all the merit out of it.'

153

The Imp and the Crust

(Adapted from a folk tale retold by Tolstoy)

A poor farmer set out at dawn to do a day's ploughing. When he reached the field he took off his coat, folded it into a neat square and placed it beside the hedge. Then he started work. He toiled for some hours in the growing heat until sharp pangs of hunger told him it was time for breakfast. He picked up his coat, put his hand in his pocket to take out his meal – a single crust of bread – and found that it was missing. 'It's been stolen!' he exclaimed. 'Never mind, whoever took the bread must have needed it badly. I hope he enjoys it.'

Behind the hedge an imp, one of the devil's pupils, snarled in disappointment. He had stolen the farmer's crust in the hope of making him swear and rage. The poor man's kind nature had beaten him. The imp flew off at once to report his failure to the devil. Old Nick angrily ordered him to use any dirty trick he could think of to change the farmer into a villain. The imp promised that he would do his level worst, and flew back to earth.

Three years later he returned, baring his pointed teeth in a grin of triumph. 'I've got him,' he told the devil. 'Come and see for yourself.' Together they winged up to earth and peeped in at the farmer's window.

Around a long table a large group were eating and drinking. From time to time the farmer refilled his guests' glasses with an amber-coloured drink. Soon the devil noticed a sly expression steal over all the flushed faces. The merry-makers spoke kind words to their neighbours but the cunning glint in their eyes showed that they were out to deceive each other. A little later they began to quarrel. Loud insults were hurled across the table. Then someone threw a punch. In an instant the room was a brawling mass of flying fists and feet. Plates smashed on the stone floor and chairs splintered under falling bodies. Finally the guests staggered to the door and reeled out into the night, one or two of them on hands and knees. The farmer, who had behaved worst of all, stood in the doorway swearing in a voice of thunder. Then, like a felled forest tree, he pitched slowly forward and sprawled in the mud.

The devil turned to the imp. 'You've done a lovely job,' he said warmly. 'It was that drink, wasn't it? What did you make it from? No, let me guess – fox's blood to make them sly, wolf's blood to make them fierce, and pig's to turn them into swine.'

'Nothing like that,' laughed the delighted imp. 'Let me tell you the whole story. I took on human shape as a farm labourer. I went to work for the farmer. He took my advice on where to plant his corn. He sowed it on low-lying, marshy ground. The sun scorched all that summer, as I knew it would. All the other farmers' corn shrivelled in the heat but our friend's grew thick and full-bodied. The next year I advised him to plant on the hillside. That summer the rain fell day after day, rotting the corn on the plain. But on the well-drained hillside our farmer's crop was a rich golden square.

Before very long his barns were bursting with grain. And then —' and here the imp smiled at his own craftiness, '— I taught him how to use the grain to make strong drink. The stuff is harmless in small doses but deadly in large ones. It seems that in every man's soul there is something of the fox, the wolf and the pig. It only needs a bottle or two to free the beasts.'

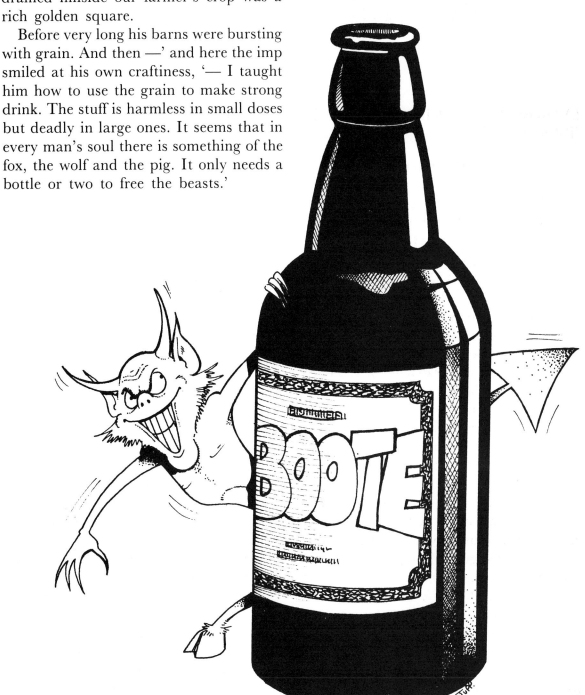

Oisin

One morning the Irish warrior Finn went stag-hunting with his son, Oisin. They were surprised to see a white horse galloping towards them, ridden by a young woman with golden hair. When she reached them Finn asked her who she was and where she came from. Her name was Niamh, she said, and she lived in the Land of the Young, where her father was king. She had come to ask Oisin to marry her. Everyone agreed that he was the finest young man in the world.

The two men looked at each other, dumbfounded. Then Oisin found his voice. Yes, he declared, he would marry the princess and live with her in the Land of the Young, for he had fallen in love with her the moment he saw her. He bade his father a sad goodbye, mounted the white horse behind the princess Niamh and sped off.

All day they rode until they reached the sea. Out over the water they galloped, their horse's hooves kicking up bursts of spray from the crests of the waves, and at last reached the Land of the Young. Oisin was dazzled by its beauty. Bright green meadows decked with sweet-smelling flowers smiled under a sun that shone every day of the year. The stones that lay by the roadside were precious ones that gleamed in many colours.

The king and queen, who looked scarcely older than their daughter, made Oisin welcome. Next day the young couple were married at a ceremony attended by all the noble lords and ladies in the land. Oisin was astonished at how youthful everyone looked. There was not a wrinkle or grey hair to be seen. Niamh explained that in the Land of the Young people grew up but never grew old.

Oisin and his young wife settled down in the palace to a life of ease and happiness. He never ceased to be amazed at a country which knew no sickness, wars, hunger or death. But after a few years he began to look back on his old life in Ireland. He remembered the excitement of battle, the thrill of the hunt, the great feasts with the Red Branch knights and the companionship of boyhood friends. Above all he longed to see his father again, for the old man, he thought, must by now be nearing his end.

One day Oisin said to Niamh, 'I must go back to Ireland again. I promise I'll return.'

Niamh nodded sadly in agreement. 'The white horse will carry you there and back,' she said. 'But there is one thing you must remember. Do not for any reason dismount from the horse. If you do, you will never return to the Land of the Young.'

Oisin gave his word that he would not dismount, kissed Niamh tenderly and saddled up the magic beast. Then off he dashed across the sea to Ireland. He rode straight to his father's castle. When he saw it his eyes opened wide in shock. Crumbling ivy-covered walls were all that remained. The great hall stood open to the skies.

Some men nearby were trying to roll a

huge stone up a hill. He rode up to them and asked, 'Where is my father, the warrior Finn?' They looked at him blankly. Then up spoke an old man: 'There was once an old king named Finn who lived in that ruined castle. But he's been dead and buried these three hundred years.'

All at once the truth hit Oisin with a force that left him numb. He had not spent three years in the Land of the Young, but three hundred. Time was different there. So everyone and everything he had loved as a boy were gone forever. Sadly he turned to go.

'Sir, please help us.' It was the old man who spoke. 'You are much bigger and stronger than we are. Will you help us roll this boulder up the hill?'

Oisin smiled at this new race of Irish-men who were little more than half his size. He bent down from the saddle and picked up the massive stone with one hand. With a flick of his mighty wrist he tossed it to the top of the hill. But in doing so his saddle-band broke and he tumbled to the ground. Suddenly his big body grew stooped and shrunken, his hair turned white and his skin went yellow and blue-veined. The horrified workers watched him wither into an ancient, blind, crippled wreck.

The white horse galloped off to the Land of the Young, leaving Oisin to live his last few miserable years in Ireland. He was not the first man to find that you can never recapture the happiness of the past, and he was far from the last.

Shirvan and the Owls

Once there lived a king named Shirvan who ruled so badly that his prime minister was often in despair. Most of the time Shirvan behaved sensibly but every now and then he would fly into a fury. Then he would do something wicked that made people forget all his good actions. One of his favourite outrages was to order all the inhabitants of a village to leave their homes. Then he would send in his soldiers to knock down every building. The prime minister longed to give him good advice but was too scared to try.

One day a man approached the king's throne to ask a favour. Before he could open his mouth Shirvan sentenced him to death. The terrified fellow protested. The king would not be moved. 'But, but you mustn't kill *me*, your majesty,' stammered the man. 'I'm a very special person. I have a skill that no one else possesses.'

'What's this skill?' snapped the king.

In a quavering voice the man babbled, 'I'm, I'm the only man alive who can understand the language of birds.'

'Liar!' Shirvan snarled.

At this point the prime minister, who had been listening with horror, implored the king to spare the man's life. Shirvan unwillingly agreed to do so. 'Make him teach you bird language, if he really understands it,' he growled.

The minister took the frightened fellow outside, where the man confessed that he knew nothing of bird-talk. He had made up the story on the spur of the moment in the hope of escaping death. The prime minister told him to go home and forget all about his shocking experience.

The king too forgot the incident until a summer evening some time later. He and the prime minister were sitting in the garden enjoying the sunset. Two owls in a cedar tree began to make their weird whooping cries. 'I say,' said Shirvan, 'did that crazy chap teach you the language of birds?'

'Well er, he made everything clear,' replied the minister, not wishing to tell an outright lie.

'Then tell me what those two owls are chatting about,' said the king.

The prime minister saw the chance he had been waiting for. 'They are two father birds. The daughter of one will shortly marry the son of the other. The father of the bride provides a dowry, just as we humans do. The bridegroom's father insists that the bride must bring seven ruined villages as her marriage-lot. It seems that owls love to take over wrecked villages. The bride's father claims that seven is far too many, for he has two other daughters to marry off.'

The king asked, 'What does the bride-grooms's father say to that?'

'He says that as long as King Shirvan is on the throne there will always be plenty of ruined villages,' answered the minister.

The king turned red with rage. 'You dare say that to me,' he hissed.

'*I* didn't say it,' retorted the prime

minister, raising his hands in a gesture of innocence, 'the owl said it.'

For a long moment, during which the king glared at him, the man thought his last day had come. Then Shirvan rose and stalked into the palace. By the next morning he was a changed man. He showed mercy to all the rascals brought before him. He announced that he would never again knock down a village, and he kept his word.